As seen in *The Wall Street Journal, Saveur, Whole Living, Edible Seattle, Smithsonian Magazine,* Seriouseats.com, Amazon.com, NPR, and *Sierra Magazine.*

Additional praise for Langdon Cook and *Fat of the Land*

"Once in a while a book crosses my desk that gives me pause, and once in a very great while, a book will resonate with me in such a way that it becomes part of my permanent collection and the recipes join my regular repertoire. *Fat of the Land: Adventures of a 21st Century Forager,* by Langdon Cook, is one of those. Part memoir, part cookbook, part field guide for the adventurous gourmand, Cook's book is simultaneously lyrical, practical and quixotic... [H]is essays paint a timeless portrait of the region, evoking its dark ambiguities as well as its brighter joys."
—Greg Atkinson, *The Seattle Times*

"Langdon Cook understands that the goal of hunting and foraging is not just to eat, but to eat well. Any city-eater can grab something at a supermarket, but to feel the thrill of grappling with lingcod or plucking dubious mushrooms gives the reader maximum pleasure—and zero pain. Provided you follow Cook's recipes to satiate your whetted appetite. As a forager with a well-trained palate, Cook knows best."
—Betty Fussell, author of *My Kitchen Wars* and *Raising Steaks: The Life & Times of American Beef*

"Cook's exuberance for the fruits of his adopted Pacific Northwest is contagious... For in Cook's eyes, foraging is not about providing only for oneself, but about building community. A good meal is meant to be shared, after all."
—*High Country News*

"Cook's detailed descriptions of the where, the how and the why of wild foraging influence more the way I think about the environment in a political sense than my plans for the weekend. The dichotomy between bounty and restriction, between poison and good health, between fear of the unknown and liberty from the tyranny of the supermarket aisle, are writ large in *Fat of the Land.*"
—WeAreNeverFull.com

"Cook, an outdoorsman, amateur naturalist and former editor at Amazon.com, first began foraging as a trailside diversion but has spent the better part of the last decade getting in touch with his inner hunter-gatherer, schooling himself in the art of 'shooting' razor clams, mapping out burn sites for signs of morels, and cataloging a veritable crisper-full of delectable weeds. That education ... proved a transformative experience for Cook, and inspired him to bring the gospel of wild food (in all of its muddy, wet, prickly and, yes, tasty glory) to the wider world."
—Salon.com

FAT OF THE LAND

ADVENTURES OF A 21ST CENTURY FORAGER

LANGDON COOK

SKIPSTONE

Published by Skipstone, an imprint of The Mountaineers Books
Printed in the United States

First hardcover edition 2009. First paperback edition 2011
14 13 12 11   5 4 3 2 1

Adaptations of the noted chapters previously appeared in *Gray's Sporting Journal*
("Silver Beach") and in *Seattle Metropolitan* ("The Inhuman").

Copy editor: Sherri Schultz
Cover design: Mayumi Thompson
Interior design: Jane Jeszeck, www.jigsawseattle.com
Cover photograph: © Getty Images/Glenn Oliver
Interior illustrations: © Isolde Maher/4 Eyes Design

This book is not intended as a substitute for professional advice or your own good
judgment. Foraging for any foods, especially mushrooms, requires significant care and
knowledge. Prevailing rules and regulations should be adhered to in any park, city,
county, state, or federal lands which you visit. The author and publisher disclaim any
responsibility for adverse effects resulting directly or indirectly from information contained herein.

ISBN (hardcover): 978-1-59485-007-3
ISBN (paperback): 978-1-59485-086-8
ISBN (ebook): 978-1-59485-397-5

Library of Congress Cataloging-in-Publication Data
Cook, Langdon, 1966–
  Fat of the land : adventures of a 21st-century forager / Langdon Cook.
    p. cm.
  ISBN 978-1-59485-007-3 (hardcover)
  1. Forage plants—Northwest, Pacific. 2. Plants, Edible—Northwest, Pacific.
      3. Fishing—Northwest, Pacific. 4. Cookery (Wild foods) 5. Cook, Langdon,
      1966—Homes and haunts—Northwest, Pacific. I. Title.
QK98.5.U6C66 2009
581.6'3209795—dc22
                    2009020053

Skipstone books may be purchased for corporate, educational, or other promotional
sales. For special discounts and information, contact our Sales Department at 800-553-
4453 or mbooks@mountaineersbooks.org.

Skipstone
1001 SW Klickitat Way
Suite 201
Seattle, Washington 98134
206.223.6303
www.skipstonebooks.org
www.mountaineersbooks.org
♻ Printed on recycled paper

LIVE LIFE. MAKE RIPPLES.

For my families,
both old and new, who gave
me the woods

TABLE OF CONTENTS

dandelion

AUTHOR'S NOTE

The Oxford Dictionary of English, one of the more modern volumes in Oxford's vast reference library, defines the verb *forage* as to "search widely for food or provisions." This is in contrast to earlier definitions that centered largely on the word's militaristic underpinnings, dating from at least the early fifteenth century, when *forrageing* had more to do with smashing an enemy and carrying off his loot. The allure of plundering and pillaging notwithstanding, my own definition adheres strictly to the contemporary interpretation. The act of foraging, by this definition, encompasses all the various modes of food finding practiced by our preagrarian ancestors, including both the hunting and the gathering.

Dictionaries aside, it seems most people, when considering the idea of foraging, place emphasis on the gathering part. My favorite description is one I heard not too long ago from another forager: he called it the act of collecting wild food *that can't run away.* Such a definition includes the plants and fungi that are implicit in the notion, not to mention slower animals like clams and mussels that are gathered rather than hunted. However, for the wide-ranging purposes of this book, I have taken the broader view, closer to that of Oxford. In the pages that follow, the forage includes wild foods that are gathered—or otherwise caught—by any means other than firearms. This includes various forms of fishing (with an angle or a spear, for instance) that some might consider to be a form of underwater hunting. The absence of firearms is not a commentary on my feelings about guns or hunting; much to the contrary, learning how to hunt larger game will probably be the next step in my ongoing education as a modern-day forager.

PROLOGUE

As a graduate student in Seattle, I met an olive-skinned Polish-Italian beauty who wrote poetry and watched birds. She took me for a spring hike in the cool evergreen forests of the Cascade Mountains. I followed her movements in the woods as she bent to identify wildflowers along the trail and cocked an ear toward the mating calls of hidden thrushes. I was bowled over by her deep connection to nature.

The natural world had always been a comfort to me. My grandparents introduced me to the swamps of Florida as a kid, and the woods near our suburban Connecticut house were a place of endless hideouts and exploration. But as I got older, these places grew more distant. Then I moved to Seattle—a city surrounded by woods, mountains, and water—and found myself seated in a literary theory class next to Martha, a grown woman who nevertheless decorated her walls with posters of local birds and flowers. I was in my early twenties, living by myself for the first time, and while Martha may have been excited to meet someone who appreciated Whitman and could identify a ruby-crowned kinglet by ear, other gaps in my education quickly began to reveal themselves to her. In four years of college in rural Vermont, I'd cracked open the great books of literature but never cracked an egg. Cooking meant heating up a box of mac 'n' cheese or opening a can of chili. I didn't know what garlic was and couldn't chop an onion. What Martha first saw in me, I cannot exactly say.

After her first night at my apartment, I offered the next morning to cook her up what I considered a breakfast delicacy. My kitchen was tiny, more like a hotel kitchenette. I waved a dull Goodwill knife in the air: "Stand back, Marty, and let the chef work his magic." Martha watched—with intrigue and then carefully disguised horror—as I pulled a package of Hormel Canadian bacon from the nearly bare refrigerator with a flourish, along with two plastic-wrapped slices of Kraft American cheese. "Taste one of my signature homemade egg muffins," I said suavely, "and you'll never eat at McDonald's again."

She picked up the bacon package with thumb and forefinger and looked at it as if studying a stool sample. "I don't do McDonald's," she said dryly.

I was confused. "What do you mean?" I stammered, struggling to open an English muffin with a fork. "Everyone eats there sometimes. Two billion served."

"Not me. I'm not counted in that tally." With that she disappeared into the bathroom for a shower, cleansing herself of the thought of my cooking altogether, and left a few minutes later.

Luckily I got another chance. During a wet weekend of backpacking along the wild Pacific coast, we came upon what Martha declared a culinary bonanza. Like a person possessed, she dropped her pack and started rummaging through her pockets, looking for a knife. "The fruit of the rain," she kept saying, explaining that here beside the trail was a species of parasitic mushroom making a slow meal of a half-dead hemlock. Commonly known as chicken-of-the-woods, the edible fungus looked like dozens of golden Frisbees stacked vertically along the trunk of the tree. With a predatory vigor I had never seen before, Marty hacked off the freshest blooms and stuffed them into her pack.

Back in town, I offered to cook up the mushrooms myself. Recently I had perfected one of the mainstays of the graduate student cookbook: the stir-fry. With potluck dinners and other gatherings happening just about weekly, I was discovering that it was important to know a few dishes that I could reliably feed to my fellow students and professors, all of whom were older and more experienced in the kitchen. Martha warily agreed, and we invited another couple over to join us. True to their name, the chicken-of-the-woods mushrooms were firm and sautéed up nicely with garlic and ginger. I added onion and peppers and splashed on some soy sauce and sesame oil before serving them over rice. Everyone dug in. The food was warm and delicious. Our guests asked for seconds. "You ought to come diving with us for Dungeness crabs," they said. "There's nothing better than a meal you've foraged yourself. Living like a hunter-gatherer is good for the soul."

And so began my education as a forager. Though I didn't come from a family of hunters—we had put down our weapons long ago—I soon learned from my hikes around the Northwest that it was still possible to gather a good meal in the wild, even in the city. I'd been a fisherman since my late teens and was always a big eater, but now a much wider world of outdoor adventure and culinary exploration was beginning to reveal itself. Crabbing sounded like a good idea. Spending time outside and living off nature's bounty appealed to me. There was something romantic about freshly foraged food.

Never again, I vowed silently, would I do something as unimaginative as try to copy a fast-food recipe. In between bites of stir-fried chicken-of-the-woods, Marty and I stole glances at each other. Her plate was soon clean, and her sated smile told me I was forgiven.

WINTER

razor clam

HONEY, GET THE GUN

AS STIRRING AS the fake snow, choo-chooing model trains, and piped-in carols were on a December afternoon on the coast, we hadn't braved the local Ace Hardware's one-day sale and its crowd of wild-eyed shoppers to cross items off our Christmas lists. While Martha scanned a glass display case of utility knives, I left with my new gun and went next door to the liquor store, where I purchased a bottle of dark rum. Outside, the sky was unseasonably clear. It would be cold tonight.

We had come to the Pacific coast of Washington on a mission, entering Ocean Shores like everyone else—through a pair of stone pillars that funnels traffic onto a little peninsula north of Grays Harbor, the shallow estuarine bay first described by Captain Robert Gray, who also "discovered" the Columbia River fifty miles to the south. This is David Lynch country, the coastal equivalent of Twin Peaks. Southern California it is not—although certain town fathers (or developers, at any rate) must have thought they could market it as such when they bought Point Brown peninsula from the family that owned it in 1960. There are still no traffic lights in this hamlet of a few thousand souls, yet the boulevards are broad—three lanes in each direction at the main crossroads, anticipating a crush of cars that never quite materialized and resulting in confusing twelve-way-stop intersections that flummox the region's notoriously defensive drivers.

Hotels and shopping malls seem determined to be anywhere else: there's a Nantucket Square, a Canterbury Inn, and a Polynesian Resort. One of the two main drags is named Chance à la Mer.

Martha was delighted to see that there was a bowling alley, and instructed me to drop her off so she could indulge some retro Jersey Shore fantasy from her youth while I poked around. Beyond the downtown I found a carefully platted community with empty cul-de-sacs, streets leading to nowhere, and a lot of scrub. Vacation houses along the beach, with the odd exception of a jaunty aquamarine-painted bungalow or a shingled Cape Cod–style cottage strung with colorful buoys, were drab and battened down with plain storm windows and non-fussy, out-of-the-box architectural details for handy weatherproofing. Many of them didn't even bother with decks overlooking the Pacific. The ocean, for that matter, was still far away, way out there beyond tall dunes and down a broad, sloping beach. Most of the time it isn't even visible. The houses get pounded all winter, and even in summer they're usually shrouded in a cold and salty fog until noon.

But on certain weekends during the off-season, the beaches come alive. At least, at dusk they do. Like extras in a topsy-turvy Annette Funicello romp, crowds come out dressed in their finest North Coast beachwear: parkas, rain jackets, fleece, long johns, hats and gloves. People line the beach as far as you can see in either direction, thousands of them. If there's a bikini, it's of the undergarment variety. Everyone carries lanterns and flashlights, and they're armed to the teeth.

Joining the crowd out on the beach an hour before low tide, it didn't take me long to draw a bead with my new gun. I aimed and commenced to digging. It was open season on razor clams.

Like noodling for flatheads in the Delta, running a sap line in New England, or dropping a baited hook through a hole in the ice in the Great White North, digging razor clams is a peculiar and time-honored expression of regional identity. Being a transplant, I suppose I didn't catch on to this fact right away. Martha and I were both from the East Coast. Our idea of a good clam was straight out of the boardwalk clam shack. They don't do clams like that out here, we figured. We didn't even know what a razor clam looked like.

Golden-hued and shaped like a straight-edged razor, the Pacific razor clam (*Siliqua patula,* for "open pod") makes its home along the sandy, storm-tossed beaches of the Northwest, from Pismo Beach, California, to the Aleutian Islands of Alaska, where they earn a living filtering plankton, particularly a species of diatom known as *Attheya armatus,* which lives in the surf and can turn the water black like an oil slick if present in sufficient numbers.

Breeding is a haphazard affair. Razors are disciples of the "hit or miss" method of reproduction; they broadcast eggs and sperm on the sand in large quantities, and fertilization is strictly by chance. The young clam begins life as a free-swimming larva until its shell begins to harden, whereupon it burrows into the clam beds of the intertidal zone, anywhere from a few feet above the low-tide mark to a half mile out at sea, and settles down to grow into the big, meaty adult that has enticed humans—and many other predators, including grizzly bears—for millennia. The fully grown shell is typically between three and six inches long, though larger specimens up to eleven inches have been found in the northern reaches of its range. In Washington, a razor clam of six inches is considered a prize (one fisheries biologist told a local paper that he had never collected one larger than six and a quarter inches, although a friend of his claimed to have found one six and a half inches long and three inches across, a real lunker). Factor in that the soft body of the clam extends well beyond the shell in its natural, unthreatened state and you get an idea of how meaty they can be. A single good-sized razor clam might have more usable flesh on it than a small quail.

Which brings us back to the "gun." An ingenious device. Nothing more than a humble length of PVC or metal pipe with a handle attached. It's used to unearth the wily razor from its lair beneath the sand. Striking a pose like a hard hat–wearing jackhammerer, the clam digger works his tube several inches down into the wet sand before closing a vent on the handle. With suction he can now pull up a core of sand—and, if he's skilled, a razor clam secreted within. It's not as easy as it might seem. Razor clams are fast. Though reports vary, one researcher clocked a razor burying itself at a rate of an inch per second. At that pace, I refuse to entertain snide remarks about fair chase. These tubes are by far the weapons of choice for extracting the clams. Wherever you go on the coast you hear clammers referring to their guns, but in truth the term was originally coined to describe a small, angled shovel invented in the 1940s and used for the same purpose. Naturally, as with any other long-standing tradition, there are old-school clammers who will eagerly correct you if you call your tube a gun. But everyone does, and so did I.

The sun was dropping fast. People and their vehicles lined the beach. (The outdated tradition of allowing cars and trucks to tear up and down the beach, spewing exhaust fumes and leaving waffle-patterned tire tracks in the sand, lives on in parts of Washington State.) Already a swath of clam bed was in disarray, the diggings heaped on the hardpan sand like the work of giant earthworms. Clam diggers were whooping it up. "Limits for everyone!" I heard a shaggy-looking logger type bellow through his beard. Apparently it was a good crop. After failing to hit pay dirt on my own first few pulls, I walked a little ways to find an unmolested stretch of beach. I wouldn't say that panic was setting in, but already I was getting a ghostlike taste of fried clam on my tongue, a tantalizing reminder of the empty mesh bag that hung limply from my belt. It's okay, I assured myself, I'm new to this. How hard can it be? As if answering my own question, there in the wet sand, clear as my thumb, was what I had been looking for: a *show*—the round, quarter-sized impression made by a clam's siphon as it lies buried in the sand—and then another. The telltale signs of razor clams were all around me, X's on a treasure map. I took aim with the gun and worked it into the sand. The sand gave way easily—until I heard the sickening crunch of breaking shell. Smashed bits of razor clam came up with my core. By law I was required to keep what was left of the bifurcated bivalve. My next pull repeated the carnage. I dropped the mangled carcass sheepishly in my bag.

Nearby a guy danced around on the flats with a mesh sack heavy with clams. He was beaming with good fortune. "Excuse me, but..." I held up the broken fragments of my first two clams. The man chuckled, his mustache twitching. "Don't talk to me. I'm just holding the bag," he said, with almost too much lip-smacking anticipation in his voice for me to bear. He pointed to a young woman in purple rain pants who was bent over her tube with fierce intent. "Talk to my daughter. She knows all. Here"—he grabbed my elbow—"I'll bring you over to her so she doesn't think you're some kind of stalker."

The daughter, preoccupied with her own hunting, was slightly embarrassed at my ineptitude. Obviously I didn't strike her as either a stalker or serious competition on the clam beds. "Not much to it," she said, looking at me doubtfully. "Not really. You just dig. Don't be afraid of getting dirty."

Dirty! Did she think I was afraid of getting dirty? Did I look like someone who was determined to stay clean? "Of course," I said. "But how do I avoid...um...wastage?" I was using the term preferred by the Fish and Wildlife authorities. It sounded suddenly pedantic.

"You mean smashed clams?" She assured me it happened to nearly everyone.

They say never turn your back on the ocean, and as a rogue wave crashed the party and sent clammers scrambling for higher ground, I now understood why. Rushing water hit me at the knees and flooded my rubber boots. The North Pacific is unmerciful to those who don't follow the rules, and sometimes it's equally unkind to those who do. Signs up and down the beaches warn swimmers (even with fifty-degree temperatures, there are still those insistent on a dip) of the dangers of the powerful surf, riptides, and—unique to this neck of the woods—errant widow-maker logs, escaped from logging operations, that roll in without notice. With soggy feet, I made my way back up the beach through darkness with a hard-won limit of clams, some of them in pieces but others big and whole and glorious. My cold, wet walk reminded me of a great Henry Weinhard's beer commercial from a few years back. A bunch of young slackers are on the dunes drinking beers. Goatees, a lot of grungewear. "Here come the hotties," one announces. Cut to a shot of the windswept beach with a cold, gray ocean backdrop and a bunch of young women—not half-clad but in so many layers of foul-weather gear that each one looks like nothing so much as the Michelin man.

Marty was waiting for me at the campsite with a bucket of seawater for the clams, a blazing fire, and hot rum toddies on the stove. "Was it worth it?" she asked rather ambiguously, eyebrows arched. In the past, it was true, I had been content to stay closer to home and dig up a limit of another smaller yet more abundant species, the nonnative Manila clam, which was established in Puget Sound early in the last century. The limit on Manilas was forty per day. They're easy to find and delicious in a hearty *pasta alle vongole*, or clam pasta, which Martha had taught me how to make and which I now insisted on calling by its Italian name. Razor clams, on the other hand, have a more blue-collar, Northwestern appeal. No French or Italian spellings here, thank you. These are clams for the deep fryer, the clams that Northwest grandmothers make into chowder. As cultural icons, they pre-date floating bridges, the Space Needle, and cheap electricity. And to see an old-timey picture of the hordes on the beach digging clams is to be confronted with not only an ocean of plaid flannel but a history of hunting and gathering that dates back 10,000 years. A limit of razor clams didn't mean a lot of fancy work in the kitchen, either. Even today, there are only a handful of recipes that one sees again and again: fried razor clams, spaghetti with razor clam sauce, razor clam chowder, and let's not forget razor clam fritters (with the secret ingredient in one well-known recipe being crushed cheddar cheese Goldfish crackers).

This is all a way of saying that razor clams are very much a local delicacy. It's only natural, then, that the good ol' days of razor clam digging are long gone. You can thank Grandma for that squander, too. Like so many other wild foods, the resource was depleted by overharvest and disease. In Washington State you could dig razor clams nine months out of the year until not that long ago, which translated into a recreational harvest of between six and thirteen million clams annually. Now the harvest is carefully managed, to say the least. You get as few as fifteen to thirty-five days, with a limit of fifteen clams per person per day. (Oregon has taken a different approach, with a more wide-open season—and a poorer catch rate as a result.)

If all this weren't bad enough, there's another, more recent concern facing clam diggers: domoic acid, which can drive seabirds crazy and make humans forget what they ate for breakfast—or worse. The toxin was first discovered in Pacific shellfish in 1991 and led to immediate harvest closures. Razor clam digging in Washington was banned for a year. While domoic acid doesn't seem to bother the fish and shellfish it infects, in humans and other animals high up the food chain it enters the brain and warps nerve signals. The human illness is known as amnesic shellfish poisoning. Symptoms include headache, dizziness, confusion, loss of short-term memory, motor weakness, seizures, cardiac arrhythmia, and coma. High doses can even lead to death. There is no antidote. The toxin is responsible for several deaths in North America. In 1998, four hundred California sea lions were killed by domoic acid. It is also now believed that domoic acid was responsible for the "stranger than fiction" event that inspired Alfred Hitchcock to make *The Birds*: in the summer of 1961, hundreds of sooty shearwaters, a pelagic species that eats mostly fish and comes ashore only to breed, invaded the town of Capitola, California. The mad birds attacked people, crashed through windows, and wreaked havoc. These days state biologists must regularly test shellfish samplings from up and down the coast before they can announce an opening.

The next morning I awoke to discover just how much of a rookie I truly was. Masked robbers had invaded our camp during the night. The muddy imprints of little paws drew larcenous arabesques atop the picnic table and benches—the scene of a wild barn dance under the moon. Half-eaten razor clams, pilfered from the bucket, lay strewn across the ground, a dozen of them. Martha convinced me that there would be no salvaging partially eaten and pawed-over razors. "They have diseases, you know," she explained to me carefully, as if I were a simpleton.

"Yeah, but…"

"And what if they pooped on your clams? They don't wash up before dinner, do they? They didn't raid our stash of antiseptic wet wipes, did they?"

"Uh-huh." I didn't like these rhetorical questions, but there was no stopping her.

"They may be fastidious little brutes, but you wouldn't want to chance eating clams played with by feces-encrusted raccoons."

I looked at the ruins on the ground, then balefully at Martha.

She smiled the exasperating smile of the sensible. "Chance à la mer."

That evening, toting my gun, I went back out for my second limit. Low tide was scheduled for 6:11 PM, well after sunset. This time the clams were more persnickety about dropping clues to their whereabouts. I wandered around without seeing a single show. As luck would have it, I was working a stretch of beach next to a guy who clearly knew what he was doing. Even though the clam shows, for whatever arbitrary reason, were few and far between, this fellow didn't care. He stalked them anyway, shifting into some deeply atavistic mode that I couldn't even begin to understand. Maybe he had X-ray vision. While I looked high and low for a show, he took one or two big steps with his gun and then—kerplunk!—he was at it again, rocking his tube into the ground and nonchalantly pulling up a core of wet sand.

Each time, his two young daughters protested their father's uncanny skill. "I don't see it," they'd say skeptically, to which he'd grunt and give the core a little kick with his boot, the wet cylinder of sand losing its shape and falling apart to reveal the wriggling snout of yet another giant razor clam. "Eek!" the girls would squeal with delight, and he'd reply, "Go ahead. Pick it up." I could only surmise that in giving his wife and daughters the pleasure of the final capture, he was able to extend the fifteen-clam limit to each family member, giving his little consortium an actual limit of sixty clams. Sixty! I wanted to crack this guy over the noggin with my gun.

The pinch of envy reminded me of competitive morel hunting and salmon fishing. It was a debilitating emotion that could only lead to further moral dissipation and a general funk. Should I walk away immediately and find a new patch of beach? Confess my ineptitude and beg for help? Better to watch and learn, I decided. Unlike many of the clammers around us, who roamed far and wide in search of the elusive show, this mollusk clairvoyant was digging in a fairly contained area. Each time he successfully dug up a clam, he moved a couple of steps and was into another one. I slowed down and studied the sand. Where there was a tiny aberration—not really the dimple of a show, just the slightest indentation—I dug anyway, and came away with a nice-sized razor. While pulling up my core, I watched the sand around me change color as the surrounding moisture leached into the tube. The sand turned from dark to light and exposed two more indentations that had previously escaped my eye. I marked these before retrieving my clam and then went back to them. Again, a couple more clams in the bag.

It was well after dark when I made my limit, but it was a limit, by God, and I could go home with head high. The light of my headlamp led me up to the dunes and along a trail to the campground, where hundreds of clammers in RVs were already cooking up their catch and clinking celebratory bottles of beer.

Truth be told, Martha is a little bit squeamish. The huge clams in our bucket scared her the whole drive home with their long, lolling necks probing their captivity—and those muscular feet that seemed capable of burrowing right into your palm if you picked one up. She didn't like the idea of having them in her basement either, so I went ahead and cleaned them while she was out. Unlike most clams, razors must be cleaned before eating. I poured boiling water over the clams for ten seconds or so, as instructed by the state Fish and Wildlife brochure; and sure enough, the golden shells started popping open, revealing their treasures. Next I removed the meat, which came away easily enough. With a pair of scissors I nipped off the tough black tip of the siphon and slit the clam from neck to foot in order to remove the "dark parts"—the gills and palps. I also butterflied the clam's foot, or digger, removing a transparent tube known as the crystalline style, which acts as a sort of tenderizer, breaking down the hard shells of diatoms in its diet with digestive enzymes. The foot is the juiciest part of the clam. This took a half hour or so, and when I was done I had a colander full of glistening clams, creamy translucent and fresh as could be. I scooped up handfuls and let them slide through my fingers back into the colander, imagining to what purpose I could put each handful. I felt like Daffy Duck in *Ali Baba Bunny* when he finds the sultan's treasure trove: "I'm rich. I'm wealthy. Yahoo. I'm comfortably well off." I, too, wanted to do the backstroke among my pile of glittering clams.

Let me just say this about the golden razor clam: if you enjoy a cup of chowder now and again or a greasy plate of fried longnecks at the clam shack, you don't know what you're missing. At first I was happy enough to dig the more common varieties that lay just beneath the surface of Puget Sound's clam beds:

littlenecks, Manilas, and the like. Steamed with a little white wine, parsley, and garlic, these make excellent table fare in their own right. But when it comes to true American comfort food, the razor clam is king. We're taught that bigger is not necessarily better; not so with the razor. A single limit of fifteen clams was enough for a kettle of chowder and a fried clam dinner, with an appetizer portion of leftovers for the freezer to boot. Size, in this case, has zero impact on flavor; my trophy clam, six inches on the nose, was just as tender and sweet as the smaller ones. The chowder we made was like none I had ever tasted, ebullient with the essence of clam rather than overwhelmed by potato or cream, the experience not unlike gulping down raw oysters: a delirious taste of the sea. And the fried clams? You haven't really eaten this venerable seaside basket meal until you've tried fresh razors. The flavor knocked us out. To think, we had wasted all this time not eating fresh razor clams. It was enough to make us blubber in our baskets. Until we remembered the end of that classic Bugs Bunny episode, when the duo, now penniless, has been banished from the sands of Arabia: "Well, here we are! Pismo Beach and all the clams we can eat!"

RAZOR CLAM CHOWDER

To make my first Razor Clam Chowder, I had to ask around a lot. As a youth, I worked at a Martha's Vineyard restaurant famous for its chowder—whipped, creamy, and so thick you could spread it on toast points. But that miraculous, float-a-cherry-on-top creaminess didn't come from any particular technique or wizardry in the kitchen; it came from giant cans labeled "Chowder Base." My grandmother Mimi used to make a New England–style fish chowder when all the relatives gathered on Cape Cod for the Fourth of July weekend. I can remember watching epic tennis matches between Björn Borg and John McEnroe while slurping down the chowder with a lot of oyster crackers thrown in for good measure. But once Mimi was gone, the recipe was too. I've tried to re-create it with both clams and cod, and after consulting with numerous cousins, aunts, and uncles over the years I'm pretty sure I've almost got it. A key ingredient is thyme. And don't even consider making this chowder without pig .

> ⅓ pound salt pork, cubed, or 4–5 strips of quality bacon, diced
> 1 large onion, sliced into wide half-moons
> 2–3 cups peeled and cubed red potatoes
> 3 tablespoons butter
> 3 tablespoons flour
> 1 quart chicken stock or clam juice, or a mixture of both
> 1 heaping teaspoon dried thyme
> Salt and freshly ground black pepper to taste
> 1 pint heavy cream (or half-and-half)
> 2 cups chopped razor clams (with as much juice
>   as can be salvaged)

Sauté salt pork or bacon in heavy pot over medium heat until crispy; remove with slotted spoon and set aside on paper towel. Sauté onions a few minutes in pork fat; add potatoes and cook, stirring occasionally, until potatoes start to brown slightly. Remove onion-potato mixture for later. Melt butter in same pot and slowly mix in flour to make a roux. The roux is ready when it starts to color up, turning a faint yellowish and then pinkish. Slowly add stock. Return onions and potatoes to pot and simmer until potatoes are tender, about 20 minutes. Add thyme and seasonings. Slowly stir in cream, then add clams and cook over low heat another 10 minutes. Taste and adjust seasonings. Sprinkle with reserved salt pork or crumbled bacon, if desired. Serve hot with good bread or oyster crackers. **SERVES 8**

DOIN' THAT SQUID JIG

SEATTLE IS A SAD, wet place in the depths of winter, after the last of the holiday bulbs has blinked out and the tinsel is boxed up and carted off. Sometimes, this time of year, I head downtown looking for a little nightlife. Tonight I drive past the Space Needle and the bars and nightclubs of trendy Belltown, past the row of shiny new biotech buildings on the waterfront, and park at the foot of the old grain terminal. Next door is the public fishing pier. The Happy Hooker bait shop is shuttering for the night, but the crowd on the pier has a high-powered halogen spotlight hooked up to a car battery and everyone is on their feet, pressed up against the railing and gibbering in a dozen different languages. Anticipation is thick. There's a shout at the far end of the pier, then cheering as tentacled beasts come flying out of the water, squirting water and ink. The squid bite is on.

I'd been thinking about squid lately because there's an Italian dish I'd heard about that was supposed to be a Christmas specialty in Venice, a dish with cuttlefish, which is a close relative of the squid. It seemed so over the top to me, and somehow—just for symbolic reasons—so antithetical to the usual red and green and white of the season, that I just had to try it. In Italy they call it *risotto nero con seppie*—black risotto with cuttlefish. Black because of the ink. There aren't too many jet black foods out there, certainly not as a main course.

Though another Christmas had come and gone with the inevitable nod to a sleep-inducing roast turkey, I resolved on New Year's Eve to learn the secrets of risotto and mentioned my resolution to Marty. I told her I was determined to make a feast that would impress even her relatives in the old country.

Not that I would be seeing any of these relatives. They live in Italy, in the shadow of Vesuvius. But I liked to think we would go over there one day, maybe even for good. Learning a new language would be the least of our difficulties, and yet the thought of all those regions—Veneto, Liguria, Campania—each with its own character and cuisine, made it all seem like a worthwhile venture. I liked to imagine the day we met Martha's relatives, how we would visit the cemetery where her people were laid to rest, and then, after stumbling through ancient ruins and meeting one person after another in town with the same last name, Silano—Martha's name—we would return to the family casa. In my fantasy I needed to be prepared. They would be welcoming in the Italian tradition. I would offer to help in the kitchen. "You cook?" "Sì." Well, sort of.

More squid plopping into buckets woke me from my impossible reverie. I was missing the bite. But before I could occupy an open slot along the rail, a tiny Cambodian woman, her face a welter of wrinkles, beat me to it. She looked up at me with an enigmatic smile before turning her attention back to the water below. "Gotta be quick, Bro," someone called out down the line. He stepped aside to give me a little room, and again, before I could claim the spot, the same woman snuck in like a California parker, this time letting loose a string of what I took to be sarcastic Khmer invective. My would-be ally on the rail snickered. "She's going for the spotlight, Bro." As everyone knew, the best action was right where the luminescence hit the water. A few casts later and she was on the move again, a moth closing in on the bright light at the center of the squid-jigging universe. This time I jumped into the vacancy before another opportunistic jigger could move. I had my crummy trout rod with me, a gallon bucket, and a pocketful of lures, known as squid jigs. Shaped like a miniature cigar with a circular fan of hooks at one end, the squid jig is a happy marriage of form and function. The hooks aren't what you might think. They radiate outward like the ribs of an umbrella, more than a dozen J-shaped hooks that are not meant to impale so much as to entangle. The squid fastens onto the jig and is reeled in before it can escape. Jigs come in many different colors, most popularly glow-in-the-dark shades of green and pink.

When the bite is on, squid jigging looks easy, though like anything else it's a skill that takes practice to learn. First the squid jigger needs to figure out how deep to fish his lure. Then comes the jig itself: the wrist-flicking motion of the rod that makes the lure dance tantalizingly up and down. When a squid latches onto the lure, a barely perceptible twinge runs up the line, along the rod, and into the neural receptors of the squid jigger's fingers. So it is with most fishing, but the strike of the squid is subtle, to say the least, which is why jiggers are constantly jigging, like action painters covering a huge canvas. Some jiggers think the squid waits until that imperceptible moment between the jig's falling and rising to attack while the glowing lure is hanging in midwater and vulnerable; others say the squid attacks on the downbeat. Still others insist the squid isn't attacking at all—it's loving, they say. The idea is to pull up just as the squid has wrapped itself on the lure. Then it's stuck and hurtling toward the surface, with the weight of the water keeping it pinned on the jig. As you look down the row of jiggers, the movement of rods bending up and down has its own mechanical if somewhat disjointed rhythm, like a contraption from the earliest days of the assembly line.

The kid next to me was from Nicaragua and dressed in an Oakland Raiders windbreaker. I used to see kids in Raiders jackets on my corner when I lived in San Francisco. Too poor to buy proper gang jackets, they settled for the ready-made toughness of the one-eyed pirate, flashing their colors on that corner

for a year of intimidation and petty crime before a rival gang's
midnight drive-by ended their turf claim. The Raider introduced
himself as Victor. Victor was hauling up dinner like some kind
of squid Svengali.

"Bro, you gotta get the technique right," he said to me, taking pity on my empty bucket. Yeah, yeah, I knew about the
technique. It wasn't like I was a novice, though admittedly I was
a little bit rusty. I hadn't been squid jigging since the previous
winter.

I brought the rod tip up and let it sink. Just as I thought
my jig was at the bottom of its stroke, I lifted up again. A nearly
impalpable tug vibrated up the line and through the tip of my
rod, enough so that my fingers started reeling before my mind
even registered the impulse. The squid broke the surface and
shot out a powerful stream as if from a water pistol. Victor side-
stepped to avoid the ink that came next.

"*Calamar*...a nice one!"

"Not bad." I shook the nine-incher off the jig and into my
bucket, where it slithered around, turning the outraged colors
of an electric revolving billboard. Like its relatives the octopus
and cuttlefish, the squid is considered one of the most intelligent
invertebrates around, more brainy than many high-rung animals
with backbones. I tried to put this fact out of my mind. On my
next cast I had another one. "That's it," Victor said approvingly.
"You wanna make it sexy-like. The squid wants to get busy with
your jig." Though young Victor here was something of a guru
with the squid jig, I was pretty sure he was wrong about the
motivation of the fearsome mollusks. I didn't buy into the theory
that the squid was trying to mate with my jig. It was a voracious
predator, no doubt about it.

Squid move under the cover of darkness, invading the shallows
at night in large schools, synchronized and working in tandem.
With a supernatural mode of communication—something out
of *Close Encounters*—they talk to each other by changing colors

at will and scrolling mesmerizing patterns across their supple bodies. Coming in from deeper waters to feed and spawn, they employ jet propulsion to overtake their marks.

The many species of squid are marine cephalopods (Greek for "head-foot") within the phylum Mollusca. To those of us higher up the food chain, they're also called calamari. They're distinguished by eight arms and two tentacles, which they use to grapple prey into parrotlike beaks to be torn apart and devoured. Unlike many other mollusks, they've lost their hard shell over evolutionary time, with most of their body mass consisting of a soft mantle and a pair of winglike fins for maneuvering. Their eyes are large and highly developed. But perhaps the most interesting thing about the squid—if you can get past the suction cup–equipped tentacles, crushing beak, vertebrate-like eyes, and three hearts—is that wonderful epidermis of theirs, constantly reacting to stimuli by changing colors and patterns in a way that can be described only as trippy. This effect is achieved by chromatophores, cells that both contain pigment and reflect light. A chameleon that changes from brown to green to match its environment is using chromatophores. The function in squids, cuttlefish, and octopuses is far more advanced, verging on a sort of visible language shared by the cephalopods.

But the part of their anatomy that most interested me was the ink sac. As any first-grader knows, a squid can confuse and elude its enemy by squirting a cloud of inky black fluid into the water from a gland in its mantle—the same ink used to turn white risotto black and impart it with an unparalleled flavor of the sea. Though the ink can be ordered from specialty food shops, I planned to harvest my own.

The squid we were after was the Pacific squid (*Loglio opalescens*), also known as market or opalescent squid. Pacific squid inhabit the eastern Pacific from Baja to Alaska, and can occasionally be found in staggering numbers at the right time and place. They lay their eggs in protected sheaths on sandy bottoms, sometimes covering acres of the substrate. Here's a description given by a Washington fisheries biologist who discovered spawning beds near the Port Angeles city docks: "That underwater scene looked as though someone had carpeted a party room with millions of clusters of small, milky white balloons. The egg capsules, which were spotted over several hundred square feet of the harbor bottom, formed mats as thick as two feet." Soon after hatching, the young must learn to hunt for themselves, and not long after that they begin to school and form shoals that move into shallower waters at night to feed—where the squid jiggers congregate.

Squid jigging is an ancient art with a hallowed past. The Japanese jigged for squid centuries ago using lures carved from deer antlers and painted bright colors. Mediterraneans have been squid aficionados since long before squid-ink risotto was a favorite Christmas dish, before there were even Christians. Chinese immigrants in California were the first to fish for Pacific squid, in Monterey Bay in the 1860s. Italians followed them at the turn of the century, and now there is an active commercial and recreational fishery. Sport fishing for squid in Puget Sound has blossomed since 1978, with the building of public piers in Edmonds, Seattle, and Tacoma.

After mushrooming and clam digging, squid jigging might be one of the most inexpensive ways to get a gourmet meal. You don't need a boat or a fancy fishing rod. Any cheap lightweight trout rod will do, and you can take the bus to a free public pier. It's logical that recent immigrants are some of the most devout squid jiggers at the Seattle pier. These people foraged in their homeland, so foraging in their adopted country comes naturally. Even at a market price of $3 per pound for uncleaned squid, catching your own makes economic sense. With a ten-pound limit, that's $30 saved for another use. Besides, it's a social opportunity. While downtown hipsters are closing the bars, the squid jiggers are having their own sort of party. Hearing all the laughter in different languages, I felt like I was missing out on a great joke.

I told Victor about my plans to recreate an Italian delicacy, about my need for the ink sacs above all. "I've got lots of ink, Bro. Check it out." He motioned me over to his bucket. The rapidly growing pile of squid was squirming and writhing in an unappetizing soup of inky water and slime. Thanks, I said, but I'll get my own. I planned to harvest the ink straight from the sac itself by making a precise surgical incision, a technique I had read about in an Italian cookbook. Victor had his own plans, including a cold ceviche with onions, peppers, cilantro, and a lot of fresh-squeezed lime, as well as a hot paella. He seemed a little young to me to be contemplating such adult fare. Maybe he was bored with calamari. I looked again in his bucket. He could afford to make every squid dish in the book.

For the next three hours the action came in waves, as schools of squid invaded the pier to feed on clouds of little baitfish that zigzagged in and out of the light. If someone caught a squid, there were usually several more that followed in quick succession, but overall it wasn't a banner night. The really good nights are special: near pandemonium reigns as squid are hoisted over the rail as fast as lures can be tossed in the water, with squirting water and ink everywhere, bystanders ducking, and buckets filling. Tonight's was an average catch.

And then sometime past midnight the intermittent action came to an end. Victor reeled up his line. Frankly, I was a little disappointed.

"Calling it a night? You don't have your limit yet."

Victor said it might be a couple more hours before the schools reappeared, and I believed him. He clutched himself in the cold and for the first time I could see that he had on just a t-shirt under his windbreaker, while I was wearing long johns, fleece, and a ski jacket on top of that. "In case you didn't notice, it's cold out here, Bro."

The Cambodians switched off their spotlight and loaded the car battery and wires onto a child's red wagon. They had to work in the morning. A pair of Ukrainians in Cossack hats scoffed at this idea, clinking their flasks in a toast and boasting that they'd be out all night, whatever it took to limit. I heard a man from Taiwan complain in a saucy mix of his native tongue and some choice broken English that if he left now, he'd be driving all the way home to Woodinville without a full bucket, and what's the point of that with gas prices being what they are. His wife, he added, would not be happy. So he was staying, too. The rest of us, more than a dozen in all, trudged back to the parking lot beside the grain terminal, we American foragers, our buckets swinging at our sides, and sped away in various cars. A few walked to the bus stop. I offered to drive Victor south, but he said he had a ride lined up. "You sure you don't want any ink from my bucket?" he asked me again, and I said I figured I had enough already. We said our good-byes. The public pier looked cold and desolate except for three hunched figures at the far end.

I wasn't expecting Martha to be awake when I got back to her place. It was nearly 1:00 AM. I left the bucket on the kitchen floor and started making preparations to clean my catch. She padded into the kitchen in her socks, quiet enough that I didn't hear her—until she let out a little yelp.

"What have you *brought* into this house?"

"Those are squid. Nothing to be afraid of." I tried snatching one out of the bucket to show her, but it clamped onto the rim with a couple of tentacles and wouldn't let go. Anyway, Marty was already on her way back to bed. "I don't want to see a single suction cup in the sink in the morning," she called from the stairs.

Some people would rather not know what they're eating. We order calamari in restaurants all the time. "Suction cups are food!" I called after her. I ran cold water over each squid and rubbed away the skin. The arms and tentacles I sliced off below the eyes, discarding the hard beak in the center. Next came the mantle, with its goopy insides. I salvaged what ink I could and cut the mantle into calamari rings. Nearly an hour later I looked at my cleaned squid and then the clock. There was more than enough for risotto tomorrow. I put a skillet on high heat. A little butter, a handful of squid lightly dipped in flour and I was eating the freshest calamari you can get. The next night was Chinese New Year. I had a few old packs of firecrackers lying around and we planned to celebrate with friends over an East-meets-West menu: Chinese-style calamari with dipping sauces for a starter, and then the famous *risotto nero con calamari*. I was pretty sure Martha would be over her squid fear by then. Italian cooking in particular, I had learned early on, has a soothing effect on her that results in long, couch-bound conversations, empty bottles of wine, and an ashtray filled with olive pits the next morning. Besides, cooking risotto always means a late evening anyway because you can't make it ahead of time. The squid jiggers on the public pier would be up even later, enjoying the nightlife, ringing in the Chinese New Year with a jig.

RISOTTO NERO CON CALAMARI

In coastal Italy, particularly around Venice, this is considered a traditional Christmas holiday meal despite the somewhat shocking color. But the squid ink is what makes this one. The key to tasty squid is to either flash-fry it for a more crispy, firm texture, or to cook it for an hour or more for a tender finish. If your dinner guests are into squid and you just pulled a ten-pound limit the night before, forgo the usual sides and just get deep into mollusca: fried calamari with dipping sauces to start, followed by black risotto as the main. You can pass on homemade squid ice cream.

A note about cleaning your squid: It takes patience and a strong stomach! Try not to imagine that you're handling a spent condom. The head and tentacles separate from the mantle fairly easily. On smaller specimens it's difficult to pull out the viscera without bursting the ink sac in the process, but with larger squid you can first remove a long, hard, transparent shaft called a pen (a remnant of its molluscan shell) and then slide out the viscera intact, after which you can prick the ink sac and drain its ambrosial contents into a small receptacle for later use. Should you burst the ink sac in the cleaning process, you can still recover much of the ink simply by squeezing it out of the mantle, although it will be diluted. (If you prove less than adept, there are specialty food shops online that carry small sachets of ink for decent prices.) Next, clean any remaining gunk out of the mantle's interior and peel off the skin layer. Use a sharp knife to cut the tentacles away from the head just below the eye; make sure you discard the hard beak at the center. Now you can slice the mantle into calamari rings or strips, or leave it whole for stuffing. With some proficiency, the cleaning process shouldn't take more than a minute or so per squid.

3 tablespoons olive oil
1 medium onion, diced
3 tablespoons chopped fresh Italian parsley
1 cup fresh basil, rough cut
1 cup tomato sauce
1 pound squid, cleaned and cut into rounds
1 teaspoon (or more) squid ink
2 cups Arborio rice
8–10 cups fish or clam broth
2 tablespoons butter
Salt and freshly ground black pepper to taste

Sauté onion in olive oil over medium heat until tender. Add parsley and basil, followed by tomato sauce. Stir in squid and ink; taste and add salt if desired, and cook for 20 minutes. Stir in rice and continue stirring for 5 minutes. Add hot broth one or two ladlefuls at a time, stirring constantly, until rice is *al dente*, about 30 minutes. Stir in butter. Season with salt and pepper to taste. SERVES 6

POCKETFUL OF KRYPTONITE

I EMERGED FROM the post-holiday cave yawning and patting my belly. It was true. I was getting paunchy. Years of zealous eating had finally begun to catch up with me. My family back east called me the human vacuum cleaner. At restaurants I was famous for ordering a rich appetizer—crab cakes, say, or coconut-fried shrimp—"for the table," on top of my personal appetizer, which was more likely bisque than house salad. It was a point of honor to take down the King Arthur's Cut of prime rib, too. But on our most recent trip to the steakhouse I'd ordered the Milady's Cut, earning raised eyebrows 'round the round table. When the holiday festivities came to an end—including the heavy creamfest that is our family's Christmas dinner, with its baby peas in cream, cream-infused gravy, and the pièce de résistance, cream of chestnut puree—I stepped on a scale for the first time in my life outside a doctor's office.

"Piece of crap made in China," I muttered. Martha got on the scale.

"Nope, right on target," said she of the size 2 skirt.

"Lemme see that thing."

"It's digital."

"I only do analog."

Marty beamed at me. "Time to face facts, Tubby."

Tubby! That was certainly an overstatement. I was in great

shape. I hiked and skied and played squash. Yes, I liked to eat a lot, but I'd always been something of a beanpole, with maybe just the slightest hint of beer around my midsection, a result more of genetics than of actual beer consumption. But there it was on the scale: I was my heaviest ever—twenty-six pounds heavier than my freshman college weight.

I'd always been a nonbeliever when it came to weight-loss books. For years I had to hawk these shameless moneymakers for the Internet bookstore where I worked. Each season I met with publishers at some high-end restaurant to be pitched the latest miracle diets sure to sell zillions, while we stuffed ourselves silly on the corporate dime. We ran the typical "New Year New You" promotions. Some of the books seemed downright dangerous. They insulted basic common sense. Then my mother decided to go on one of these best-selling diets. In the process of having four children over a fifteen-year span, she had accumulated a little more gravitas than she wanted. Over the phone I derided the author as a crank and gave a vaguely puritanical speech about exercise and portion control (*me* talking about *portion control*!), but when I saw her next she looked dynamite.

So now, very secretly, I initiated the gentleman's weight-loss regimen—what my friend Kenan lovingly calls the steak and martini diet. I ate a lot of meat to fill me up. I drank a lot of vodka to ease the pain. I eliminated my beloved carbs. It was easy to keep the truth from my friends. Out to dinner I would order a meat or seafood course and ignore the potatoes or rice on the plate. Incredibly, I found myself whipping up chicken Caesars for lunch. The extra pounds started to melt off. Yes, I was grumpy and unpredictable, with mood swings too sudden and erratic to duck. "But what else is new?" quipped Martha. I was also exercising much more. When I couldn't do the things I enjoyed in the outdoors, I rode a stationary bike at home. I switched to decaf and didn't drink beer for a month. By the end of week 6 I had lost exactly twenty pounds. I was within striking distance of my teens. That would be the low. In the

next few weeks I eased back into reality with one major change:
I avoided processed foods. The gentleman's diet, I explained
to Martha, was just a way to kick-start the process. Now, with
some traction, I wanted to be smart about my eating. I wasn't
into denial. Mashed potatoes called out to me like an old
friend, and I intended to reciprocate. Still, I started reading
about health and nutrition. Michael Pollan became my touch-
stone. Political screeds like *Fast Food Nation* piled up on my
nightstand.

"What about the French paradox?" I asked Martha one night
while rummaging through the kitchen cabinets.

"They really know how to get our goat, don't they?" She
looked at me with a combination of surprise and superiority.
"You're finally catching on. Let's celebrate with a glass of red wine
and a wedge of Cambozola."

That night we agreed to buy nothing that came in a colorful package. No boxes or bags or plastic tubs of food. We would
buy just whole foods and foods that were in season, with a
concession to staples like olive oil, sugar, flour, and a few other
processed items. Plus what I could forage out of the woods and
waterways. We would spend more time cooking.

And so began my fixation on the so-called superfoods.

I'll admit that the moniker "superfoods" sounds a tad Madison
Avenue. Do an Internet search and you'll discover that the term
is most often trumpeted by a legion of self-professed nutritionists who are the same witch doctors, charlatans, and quacks
responsible, in part (there's blame to go around), for all the food
confusion across the land to begin with. Martha assailed my pre-
occupation almost immediately.

"Isn't your political affiliation a capital-S Skeptic? How could
you fall into this dumb trap?"

"What trap is that?"

"The idea that you just need to eat a few so-called superfoods
to be super-healthy."

"Did I say I was going to eat just a few foods? Remember, I like everything. Well, except lima beans."

"Lima beans are the best."

"Anyway, I just want to make sure a few of these highly nutritious foods make it into my diet."

"Okay, Superman, like what?"

Well, huckleberries, for instance, for their antioxidant prowess. And wild salmon (omega-3 fatty acids). It's not too hard to get behind those two menu items. Most superfoods, however, are leafy greens—and yet we were barely into the New Year. What wild plant could I possibly find in the middle of winter? Watercress, that's what. A European invader once closely allied with snooty little sandwiches of the upper crust, watercress is now found from sea to shining sea and across much of Canada. It's loaded with vitamins C, B1, B6, K, and E, as well as iron, calcium, magnesium, manganese, zinc, and beta-carotene. In some parts of its range it's available year-round. Even in colder climates watercress can be gathered while snow is still on the ground in early March—making it one of the first fresh greens of the year. Like many superfoods, it's considered a weed in most places, and truth be told, it does have a tendency to proliferate madly in rather marginal habitats, like roadside ditches. Not wanting to ingest motor oil, antifreeze, or herbicides, I ruled out such foraging grounds, visiting instead a friend's hideaway in the Cascade foothills where a creek supplied all the watercress anyone—or anything—could eat, including a herd of four-legged foragers.

Trying to avoid bankside elk poop, however, while scooping out handfuls of watercress did not give me quite the same thrill as digging razor clams or catching squid. Luckily, as the days got longer, another early green was beginning to stir in lower elevations, one associated with danger and pain. And as it so happens, we were already close—in a manner of speaking. I was ten or eleven years old when I first made its acquaintance, while trying to field grounders and make clean throws to first. Wesley Pratt was the team prankster back then. During batting practice one afternoon, Wesley disappeared over the chain-link fence behind the backstop and down into an overgrown creek that gurgled not far from the first-base line. He was up to something. After taking my cuts at the plate, I came back to the bench. My teammates stared straight ahead at the next batter, stone-faced. I took a seat and immediately jumped back up with a howl. My backside was on fire. Everyone collapsed into paroxysms of laughter. Now I was vigorously scratching, which caused even more of a hullabaloo. Behind me, Wesley grinned impishly and held up a seemingly innocuous stalk of green leaves with his leather glove.

"What is that stuff?" I cried.

Wesley wasn't so sure himself. "I dunno, Clark Kent. Kryptonite, maybe." He'd been reading too many comics. Another boy corrected him: in the grand tradition of ballyard pranks perpetrated by gum-snapping boys of summer, I'd been nettled.

I was incredulous. I had never seen stinging nettles before, much less known of their rare talent. At that moment, red in the face and still smarting, I could hardly imagine that years later I would deliberately search out nettles, not as a gag but as food and remedy. It's an age-old paradox most appreciated by children: what's good for you is often distasteful or even painful. Think of lima beans, cod-liver oil, and household chores. Now add to the list a nettlesome proposition indeed: *Urtica dioica,* the common stinging nettle, known as devil's apron in ancient Ireland.

I was thinking about Wesley Pratt and my first brush with stinging nettles as I skulked around in a newly found patch, keeping a lookout for any joggers, dog-walkers, or other unsuspecting law-abiders. A wise man once said it is better to beg forgiveness than ask for permission. This was city property, and though my quarry was generally classified as a weed—and a belligerent one at that—I wasn't relishing an opportunity to explain my quest for locally foraged superfood to the parks superintendent. A couple of power-walkers chugged by and then a bird-watcher, who failed to notice a pileated woodpecker hammering on a snag right above our heads. Now the coast was clear, as they say. I pulled on my rubber gloves, got down in the dirt, and drew my kitchen shears. Stinging nettle soup was on the menu.

It was the first week in March and the nettles were young, less than a foot off the ground—ideal for harvest. It didn't take long before one caught me in an unguarded moment. The sleeve of my shirt had inched up just enough above my glove to reveal an isthmus of vulnerable skin at the wrist. *Ouch!* The sting, while not nearly as painful as that of a yellowjacket or fire ant, works on similar principles: tiny hairs deliver a blast of formic acid, histamine, and serotonin. What it lacks in initial impact, however, it more than makes up for in endurance. Unlike a bee sting, a brush with nettles tends to linger for several hours. But then, never did a plant hurt so good.

It turns out that stinging nettles are a very useful and beneficial plant indeed. They're not just loaded with nasty little barbs waiting to jolt the unwary—they're also packed with vitamins, minerals, and protein. One wonders how early humans, without the use of rubber gloves and food processors, were able to discern the salubrious effects of such argumentative fare. Herbalists like to use dried nettles for teas and tinctures. In olden times, stinging nettles were often used as tonics to cure consumptives. Physicians used them for centuries for a variety of ailments and to enhance the functions of circulation, respiration, autoimmunity, and digestion. A tonic of nettles was a standard folk remedy in our not-so-distant past. As with dandelions and other early greens, stinging nettles were used to transition out of the cold season, to shake off the stiffness of winter and rejuvenate the body for the outdoor working season. Consuming nettles is said to make one's hair thicker and shinier as well as clear up skin rashes. Some arthritis sufferers swear by the medicinal value of being stung by nettles. Additionally, in Europe nettle fibers were widely used to make clothing, as recently as during World War I. As a food the leaves taste surprisingly good, with a clean, peppery zing. Once dried or cooked, nettles lose their sting. Steamed, they have a consistency not unlike spinach, with excellent flavor, making them a good alternative for spring lasagnas.

Scientists are still trying to unravel the secrets of stinging nettles, yet there is no doubt that they are one of the most nutritious plants on the planet. Nettles possess unusually high mineral levels, including calcium, magnesium, iron, potassium, phosphorus, manganese, silica, iodine, sodium, and sulfur, as well as high concentrations of B-complex vitamins, beta-carotene, and vitamin C. Perhaps most famously, they are about the best source of protein in the plant kingdom. The ability to get protein from a source that didn't run away must have been very important to early humans, not to mention other protein-craving omnivores—which may explain why the nettle has evolved its formidable defense.

Foraging for stinging nettles offers the added bonus of getting outside as the winter transitions to spring. On this day the chorus of birdsong, to name one of my favorite signs of the season, was in full throat, having picked up dramatically in the past week. Sure, the robins—those overachievers of the avian world—had been singing since late January. But as I arrived at my patch, I heard roving bands of pine siskins chittering in the treetops. A mixed flock of kinglets, chickadees, and nuthatches gossiped lower in the canopy. The high-pitched bragging of brown creepers ("see-see-look-at-me") rang out through the woods. Though spring was officially a few weeks away, Indian plums were beginning to leaf out, too, with a few brave rosettes testing the air, and the first bright green leaves of spring wildflowers were unfurling out of the duff. All of this potent reawakening is part of the nettle.

Back at home, with gloves still on, I cleaned and chopped a batch of nettles for the pot. The rest I spread out on screens for drying. Though there was no evidence of a blister or even redness, the sting on my wrist continued to itch. Scratching it, I wondered what my old teammate would make of this evening's super soup course.

CREAM OF STINGING NETTLE SOUP

Here's a recipe that, though simple, never fails to impress even my most exacting guests—and it's good for you, too. One could substitute spinach for the nettles, but the cool zip of the wild greens, when combined with the heartiness of the blended potato, is what makes this soup so distinctive.

The finished soup will be sweetened by the caramelized onion while the nettles have a fresh, peppery taste that evokes the moist woodlands of their home. Later in the spring, when the days are warmer, you can omit the potatoes and cream and skip the puree step to simply enjoy a refreshing soup of chopped nettles. You can also substitute stinging nettles in your favorite spinach lasagna.

> 4 tablespoons (½ stick) butter
> 1 medium Walla Walla Sweet or yellow onion, diced
> 2 cloves garlic, minced
> 3 medium potatoes, peeled and coarsely chopped
> Nutmeg or other seasonings
> 2 cups chicken stock
> 2 cups water
> 1 large bunch stinging nettles, chopped
> Salt and freshly ground black pepper to taste
> Heavy cream

Sauté onions in butter over medium heat until caramelized. Add garlic and potatoes and cook several minutes, until potatoes have begun to brown slightly. Season to taste. Add stock and water and simmer until potatoes are tender, about 15 minutes. Add nettles, stir, and cover. Cook 10 minutes on a low boil. Puree in blender, food mill, or processor to a smooth, creamy consistency, then return to pot. Add more stock or water if necessary; check seasoning. Serve with heavy cream, which can be floated on top in an artful design. SERVES 6

SPRING

fiddlehead

FIDDLING AROUND

TWENTY MINUTES FROM my home is a broad-shouldered chunk of geography, formerly railroad logged, that comprises several foothill peaks on the western edge of the Cascades. It's a place known to city planners and public land managers as the urban-wild interface, an uneasy pillow-sharing by homeowners, government, and timber companies, not to mention bears, cougars, and—thanks to an extensive trail network—throngs of weekend warriors. When I go to this place, usually during quiet off-peak weekdays, I can wander among the salal and Oregon grape, through groves of big second-growth timber and among tiny delicate fairy-slipper orchids, and let my thoughts roam far and wide. It's hard to ask for more on the outskirts of a major metropolitan area.

Lately I've been walking the same loop trail once a week to see the progression of spring in action. I like to linger over the flora, my divining rod in the shape of a field guide. There's comfort in knowing what all those little energy-packed shoots are going to become as they push through the forest floor and unfurl their green flags. As the weeks go on and the ground warms, the first trilliums—aptly called wake-robins in some quarters—spread their three white petals and reach for the sky. They're followed by the deep crimsons and purples of the bleeding hearts, and in boggy sections the yellow hoods of skunk cabbage.

Mats of false lily of the valley carpet the trail edges, while the pink blossoms of salmonberry offer early drive-though service to hopped-up hummingbirds. An ever-shifting parade of migrant birds comes through, flashing their new colors. The eerie, ventriloquil calls of varied thrushes echo through the woods, and in clearings the plump white-crowned sparrows whistle their heralds of future sunshine, a song that can seem overly optimistic this time of year. But with the arrival of black-headed grosbeaks, western tanagers, and flocks of neo-tropical warblers, we know, despite the weatherman's insistence on more snow flurries even in the lower elevations, that spring is honestly here.

It's around this time of year, perhaps a little before the first raspy songs of tanagers, that I lower my eyes and pay particular attention to the fetal-minded shoots of ferns emerging in tight coils from last year's died-back clumps. They're called fiddleheads—named for their distinct shape, which resembles a violin's scroll. Though the mature fern fronds are toxic, the young fiddleheads of a few particular species are edible and delicious, their taste often described as a cross between asparagus and artichoke. High-end restaurants charge handsomely for this ephemeral and attractive delicacy, and few spring treats taste more of the season's contradictions: the tenderness of rebirth coupled with the wild riot of sudden new growth. As Chaucer reminds us, springtime is full of sweet violence "pierced unto the root." The older I get, the more I accept such contradiction. Taking low-elevation walks in spring is a way to keep pace with this two-faced season; eating fiddlehead ferns is a way to incorporate it into my very cell structure. And so a handful or two will go home with me as proof.

Some foragers and gastronauts get a thrill out of tasting any mystery species willy-nilly, with nary a nod to possible side effects, just the way some adults well past the age of sixteen still like to drive fast and weave in and out of traffic. Not me. I've been sickened by an exalted species of mushroom after eating it for the first time, one that didn't agree with my system for whatever

reason, and I spent the better part of a car ride later that day
making emergency pit stops. That's part of the deal with wild
edibles—they're not domesticated. They don't exist solely for our
pleasure and sustenance. They're unpredictable.

On the other hand, when do we take our circumspection
too far? While out walking the same trail the other day, I found
a nice patch of fiddleheads. They were unwinding amid a tangle
of devil's club and salmonberry along a swampy section of trail.
The proper way to forage a fiddlehead patch is to scout the fully
leafed-out ferns in summer when they're easier to identify, then
return the following spring to harvest a small portion of the new
growth. You take two or three fiddleheads per cluster, never
more than 40 percent of the total. The choicest fiddleheads come
from the ostrich fern, a tall, elegant species with fronds that
resemble the statuesque bird's tail plumes, and the smaller, more
delicate lady fern. The ostrich is particularly abundant in the
northeastern United States and across much of Canada. In my
area I'm looking for the lady, a fairly common variety with soft,
feathery fronds that grows in parks, along streams, and in moist
woodlands. But here, in this dark patch of swampy forest, I was
pretty sure I wasn't looking at the fiddleheads of a lady fern.

I was in a quandary. These delicate green beauties, curled up
in their papery sheaths, sure looked tasty. But I couldn't ID them.
As far as I knew, there were no deadly poisonous fiddleheads,
provided you cooked them well enough; however, some species
are reported to be mildly toxic, inducing dizziness, nausea, and
lethargy in those who eat them. And there's one particular species of fern, bracken, that has been proven to have carcinogenic
properties. It causes intestinal cancer in mice and has been impli-
cated in higher rates of stomach cancer in places where humans
traditionally eat it. That said, bracken fern is considered a delicacy in Japan and has been a staple of Native Americans' diets for
millennia. Many experienced foragers will argue vehemently on
its behalf; others warn against it.

I went ahead and picked a bunch of the fiddleheads anyway.

I knew they weren't bracken. They looked a lot like the sort of fiddleheads I'd found before, except for that brown papery sheath covering most of the coil. Many young ferns are protected by a film or wool-like shroud that can usually be rubbed off easily enough. Back at home, I tried cleaning a few. The sheath didn't come off as readily as I expected. These definitely weren't ladies; they were the fiddleheads of deep, unknown woods, of trolls and golems.

What to do? I emailed my findings to a foraging listserv. Recently we'd had a thread about the carcinogens in bracken fern. I quoted Marty, who's normally cautious about food but had her sights set on these toothsome-looking greens: "Everything gives you cancer these days," she'd said in an uncharacteristic fit of dismissiveness. A fellow named Green Deane, proprietor of the "Eat the Weeds" website, wrote back:

> Everything causes cancer, and the truth is we all get cancer every day. Our immune system just takes care of it. Perhaps I am getting cranky but I would trust the nutrition in a fiddlehead before the advice of a nutritionist about the fiddlehead. When it comes to food, our ancestors got along very well without the advice of nutritionists, doctors, or researchers. They ate successfully for hundreds of thousands of years, certainly tens of thousands of years. I think a no-calorie sweetener is a far greater threat to your life than a fern. Personally, my rule is if my great-grandmother would not recognize it as food I don't eat it (Cocoa Puffs, nondairy creamer, carbonated cheese food, margarine, et cetera). And stay away from doctors. They make you sick.

Cranky or not, Deane raises some good points. On the other hand, I'm a fan of science and empiricism, if not corporate nutritionism.

Later, after doing some research, I decided I had a member of the wood fern group, possibly the spiny wood fern, also known as the spreading wood fern or buckler fern. I couldn't find anything on the edibility of its fiddleheads. Apparently Native Americans ate the pineapple-like rhizome that makes up its root base. I decided to try them anyway. Just a few. Maybe one. Our ancestors sacrificed a lot of lives in the long lab test of edibility. I don't plan to join the errors in the annals of trial-and-error, but I do want to honor their courage—if only on a smaller, not so life-threatening scale.

I boiled two fiddleheads for ten minutes, changed the water, and boiled them again for several more minutes—much longer than usual. The water turned a rusty pink and the fiddleheads lost some of their deep green luster. Next I sautéed them in butter with a little salt and pepper. They tasted better than expected, with the crispy crunch of spring asparagus tops and a buttery flavor that was indeed similar to artichoke, except more substantial. Really, I wanted more. A lot more. Over the next couple of hours I monitored my reaction. I do this when eating a new species of wild mushroom, too. Everyone should try just a little of a wild edible the first time; you don't know if you're allergic, and in this case I wasn't positive about my identification, even though fiddleheads as a general rule aren't deadly poisonous.

As on other occasions, however, my imagination went into overdrive. For a moment I felt a little dizzy. Was I getting nauseous? That would be a sure sign. Then I felt tingling in my left hand. The tingling worked its way up my arm to my shoulder. Was it my heart? The other side of my brain was hollering to relax. You're psychosomatic, it said. I probably was. The next day I felt fine. No strange dreams or midnight trips to the bathroom. Of course, there's always that nagging feeling that attends wild edibles without a track record: the damage could be a slow-to-unfold revelation—then a trip to the cancer ward. Long-term effects be damned, I cooked up a whole batch the next night and ate them with a fillet of pan-fried halibut and orzo. My fiddlehead portion seemed a little small until Martha came over later and fessed up to eating some for lunch. "When I saw you still alive this morning," she said matter-of-factly, as if commenting on the weather, "I figured they were good to go." Thanks for the concern! Hope you enjoyed them!

Right around the time fiddleheads are unscrolling their green goodness, a second welcome sign of spring is emerging in another kingdom. That would be the fungal kingdom, the taxonomic home of morel mushrooms.

Morels inspire so much excitement among mushroom hunters and foodies that I almost hate to be the bearer of bad news, but I'll say it anyway: we should be careful about wherefrom these delectable fellers come. Morels have a funny way—not unique among mushrooms but perhaps most refined in the morel—of popping up in the most unusual places. It's commonplace to hear stories from mushroom hunters about searching the woods all day without luck, only to find a dozen morels right beside the car in the parking lot. Morels like uncommon ground. They fruit in flowerpots, next to sidewalks, along driveways, even in an old shoe. Construction sites, flood zones, and slash piles are all fair game. This is part of their appeal. They're surprising little buggers, the mushroom equivalent of a can of snakes.

One of their favorite tricks is to stow away in commercial mulches, then fruit in great numbers wherever that mulch meets the ground, be that a suburban garden, an urban housing complex, or an industrial landscaping beauty strip. When morel hunters stumble across such a fruiting in, say, the middle of a busy city, they're understandably filled with joy. It is with some regret that I would tell these folks to speak with the property owner first. Find out the provenance of the mulch, or whether it's been sprayed with herbicides. Mushrooms, you see, have the ability to concentrate environmental contamination, whether it be heavy metals in the soil, chemicals applied by humans, or even airborne radiation. The Chernobyl nuclear meltdown in Ukraine famously confirmed this; to this day, wild mushrooms picked in many parts of Europe must pass a radiation inspection. Recently it's been discovered that the fungi in the immediate vicinity of the meltdown have been absorbing—and scrubbing—radiation from the soil, sort of like oysters filtering salt water. I'm guessing you don't want to eat those mushrooms, but it's sure nice having them around cleaning up the mess we make.

Several years ago I found a clump of three beautiful specimens of *Agaricus augustus,* the prince mushroom, known to mycophagists far and wide as a choice edible. The mushrooms were worm-free, with caps the size of salad plates. I found them in mulch on the University of Washington campus, outside the physics building. Like morels, the prince is known for cohabitating among men. On top of that, *Agaricus* is a genus notorious for concentrating heavy metals, but I didn't know this at the time. I took the mushrooms home and cooked them up for not one but two dinners with Marty. The first night we stuffed and broiled two of the caps with a mixture of ground pork, egg, chopped parsley, sage, diced shallot, bread crumbs, and Parmesan. Besides being meaty, with a texture not unlike a portobello (same genus), the prince is notable for its hint of anise, a sweet, almondy flavor that varies in strength from patch to patch. These particular mushrooms happened to be very sweet and almondy, really too sweet for the savory stuffing I had made, so the next night we chopped up the remaining cap and stems and sautéed them with garlic, onion, and tomato in olive oil to make a simple red sauce for fettuccini. This seemed like a better use of the mushroom's singular flavor—until we read, not long after, some literature about *Agaricus* and environmental contamination. The problem in this case wasn't that the mushrooms were foraged in an urban environment—it was that they were fruiting out of a commercial mulch.

Mulch, despite its intended use, can be nasty stuff. Lumberyards will frequently convert scrap wood into mulch. Problems arise if that scrap wood, once intended for other industrial and residential uses, was treated with preservatives—oil- or water-based chemical sprays designed to limit cracking, seal out the elements, prevent termite infestations, and so on. Other types of mulches may include recycled products such as plastics.

Much hand-wringing has gone on in recent years in the recreational morel-picking community. As mentioned earlier, morels have a tendency to fruit in disturbed ground, particularly in the American West. Prolific fruitings can occur in the spring following a forest fire or logging clear-cut, or after other disturbances such as road-building or trail maintenance. Morels will even fruit in and around old campfires. Most pickers don't worry about the fire morels, but clear-cut morels are another story. Timber companies frequently pound the cut blocks with herbicides to discourage unwanted growth before replanting the next generation of trees. Selective cuts are better, since they're usually left alone after harvest, but the clear-cut morels are best avoided unless it can be verified that chemicals weren't applied.

A friend of mine called me up all excited the other day. Get yourself over to Gas Works Park, she said, there were shaggy manes everywhere. The shaggy mane is a species of *Coprinus,* a mushroom genus known for a couple of good edibles—and also for the fact that, when combined with alcohol, even the edible species can make you sick.

"Gas Works, huh?"

"Yeah, they're everywhere. But you better be quick." The other thing about the *Coprinus* genus is that it has some of the more delicate species. Shaggy manes and inky caps begin to deteriorate soon after reaching their full size. The term of art is deliquesce. In a weird form of evolutionary adaptation, they self-digest their own spore-bearing gills, becoming a soupy black mess in pursuit of reproductive success.

"I think I'll pass," I finally said. Gas Works Park, as the name suggests, is a reclaimed heavy industrial site. The nineteen-acre point on the shore of Lake Union in Seattle was used to convert coal into gas. The city bought the site in 1962 and opened the park in 1975, with the former boiler transformed into a picnic shelter and the exhauster-compressor painted over and made into one of the world's more unusual play areas. Since the mid-Eighties, parts of the park have been periodically closed for industrial cleanup. Recently, toxic sludge has been bubbling out of the ground. According to an article in the *Seattle Post-Intelligencer,* a parks employee "is responsible for walking the grounds on a weekly basis to watch for patches of tar that are then cordoned off, dug up and refilled with dirt or gravel."

No, I would do my mushroom hunting elsewhere, thanks. The days were getting warmer. There were morels to be had along south-facing slopes of the Cascades, and I had a big patch of lady-fern fiddleheads to visit. Like so many seasonal pairings, morels and fiddleheads seem made to go together. They have more than a little bit of that rejuvenating taste of spring. Sautéed together in butter or finished with a little cream and cognac, they make an earthy companion to other seasonal specialties like fresh lamb or spring chinook salmon grilled with fresh herbs.

SAUTÉED FIDDLEHEADS

As a side dish, sautéed fiddleheads make a woodsy yet elegant accompaniment to fish or meats in the spring. Prepare the fiddleheads by rubbing off the papery sheath that sometimes envelops the young, coiled shoot and clipping the cut end if it extends much beyond the coil. Blanch the fiddleheads in boiling water for a few minutes, then remove to a sauté pan and toss with melted butter and seasoning. Simplicity is the key. Don't overcook. You want the fiddleheads to be tender yet firm, like asparagus, with a little bit of crisping on the outside.

For a slightly more decadent preparation, after blanching the fiddleheads, sauté them with butter and chopped shallots for a few minutes, then finish with heavy cream and a splash of cognac or sherry. Again, don't cook too long or the fiddleheads will look more like creamed spinach. I like to pour fiddleheads in cream over flaky white fish fillets such as halibut, lingcod, or rockfish.

THE INHUMAN

DRIVE WEST THROUGH Seattle toward Salmon Bay and you pass neighborhoods of mostly single-family homes that have been gussied up to varying degrees by California and New Jersey transplants—until you land in Ballard, the seat of local Scandinavian culture. Here you can still order a plate of *lutefisk,* and until recently—and by that I mean the 1990s—if you took a place at The Sloop's bar on a Wednesday afternoon, you might find yourself wedged between an off-duty ferry worker and a commercial fisherman. The road makes a few right-angled turns the way arterials often do on the approach to water—and then you're in the parking lot of the Shilshole Bay Marina, below a green line of bluffs to the east.

Shilshole in the Duwamish tongue means "threading the needle." Why this bay-within-a-bay off the city's northwest shore bears such a name is anyone's guess, but in 1917 it made a little more sense with the opening of the Lake Washington Ship Canal, which connected the freshwater lake to the east with Lake Union and Puget Sound to the west through a series of cuts and locks engineered by Brigadier General Hiram Chittenden just before his death. The new passage to the sea lowered Lake Washington by nine feet and dried up forever the Black River. Joseph Moses, a Duwamish Indian, said of the event: "That was quite a day for the white people at least. The waters just went down, down, until our landing and canoes stood dry and there was no Black River at all." Now, every summer, sockeye salmon enter the human-made canal instead, dodging sea lions at the locks and ascending the fish ladder on their way to spawning beds in the Cedar River. It's one of the southernmost sockeye runs left of any consequence, and in a good year more than 300,000 salmon will pass by the glassed-in viewing station at the Ballard Locks on their way home.

But today was a clear and unseasonably warm morning in May and the salmon had yet to show. I met Dave in the parking lot, where I found him already naked behind the open door of his truck, hopping on one foot as he pulled on a royal blue neo-prene bootie. I suited up quickly, and then we discreetly slipped over the fence that said "No Diving," lowered ourselves down the rusty, barnacle-encrusted ladder—not an easy feat in fins—and swam out past the boat docks to the Shilshole jetty. As a point of fact, we weren't *diving* in the sense intended by the sign. Half an hour later Dave was pointing frantically, trying to tell me that a prize lingcod was no more than six feet below us, lurking in its dark cave.

We treaded water at the surface and plotted strategy. This was the netherworld—hovering between sea and sky—and I didn't like it. The swells sloshed in and out, bobbing us up and down like a strange slow-motion carnival ride, enough so that I was starting to get seasick. I also had to pee. The hood made it hard to hear, too, and my mask was fogged and disorienting. Dave spread his arms wide so I would get the message. "Big ling," he said in a nasally tone through his mask, the waves lapping at his wispy blond beard. He instructed me to look in the shadow, where I'd see part of the head sticking out. "The boy's grinning. He doesn't think you can see him." Meanwhile, the tide was going out and we didn't have much time. Soon the water would drop below the jetty and the fish would move out of the rocks to new haunts along the bottom, out of reach. I cleared my mask with a gloved hand as best I could, took a breath, and kicked down headfirst.

The first few feet were the hardest. The water, cool and glimmering in the sunlight, stretched around me like a rubbery membrane before snapping and letting me go. Schools of flashing baitfish broke apart and re-formed like balls of mercury. Beyond a certain depth the buoyancy of my wetsuit and flippers surrendered to the twenty-five pounds of weight on my diving belt and I went down as if loosed from the land for good. This is the feeling that propels the free diver, and maybe the astronaut: the ability to move through space without hindrance. It's a feeling you can't get on land, and though scuba diving offers its own pleasures, the free dive is perhaps the most stripped-down, elemental way to give gravity the finger.

I dove ten feet and coasted easily along the rocks and up to the ling's hole, careful not to get too close and spook it. But the fish was nowhere in sight. Back on the surface, Dave was waiting impatiently. Hadn't I seen it?

I admitted that I had not.

"He's right there, man."

I said I believed him.

"He's huge. You can eat ling all week. Throw a ling-and-chip party." This was one of Dave's signature meals, which he fed to his fellow graduate students every quarter. The hungry scholars loved coming over to Dave's house, knowing they would be offered fresh fish or crabs or oysters. Many of them were fluent in the convoluted wordplay of Derridean deconstructionism, yet they could barely feed themselves.

"Clear your mask," he advised. "And open your eyes." In a given year, Dave gets in more than two hundred days in the water between the Baja and Puget Sound—and yet he still manages to show up in his classroom to lead his undergraduates through Hegel and Foucault and the radical subjectivity of Shakespeare. I had long ago stopped worrying about not seeing the things he saw underwater. Dave was also a poet, and his love of hunter-gatherer culture informed his verse. Bleached bones

and spear points lived on his bookshelves alongside volumes
of Celan and Whitman. A cupboard in the living room was
like a tribute to a countrified Joseph Cornell with its dozens of
compartments devoted to nature's bric-a-brac and tchotchkes: a
shrew's skull, the preserved paw of a puma, a great horned owl's
wing. Salt water, though, was his natural element. In water Dave
was truly himself. A mutual friend once said he admired Dave
for the way he punched his way through life. Authority, rules,
stodgy academia—despite his compact size, Dave had a way of
getting in the face of anything that seemed designed to hold him
back. Which is why the water was so perfect for him. He'd pull
on a four-millimeter wetsuit, hitch up a weight belt with thirty
pounds or so, and be down underneath Puget Sound with hardly
a splash. He'd move through the water like a seal. It supported
him and gave him freedom at the same time.

I took another dive. This time I thought I might have seen an
eye in the shadow. After the third descent I was able to pick out
the whole head. I was shaking now, but not from the fifty-degree
water. "He's right there!" I burbled through my snorkel at the surface. This was the biggest ling I'd ever seen. Dave laughed. He'd
been through this a million times—a forty-inch lingcod hiding in
an impossibly small hole near the surface, waiting to ambush an
unwary perch or rockfish. "Take the shot," he urged.

I dove a fourth time, now with my pole spear—also called
a Hawaiian sling—cocked and ready. The sling is a simple tool.
The shaft is four or five feet long. On one end is a sharpened,
three-pronged steel trident; on the other is a loop of high-tension
surgical tubing. To "load" the spear, you simply grasp the tubing
in the cradle of thumb and forefinger and move your hand up the
shaft and grip it behind the points, the surgical tubing now taut
and stretched to the limit—an advanced rubber-band projectile.
The distance of your shot is the length of your outstretched arm
plus the length of the spear shaft, or about eight feet. Realistically,
though, you need to get within a few feet of your prey to strike
successfully, and this is especially true with lings.

Long and snakelike, with a large mouth of teeth, the ling is
built to seize other fish in its powerful jaws after short explosions of speed. Sometimes they behave like eels, bursting out of
holes to grab their prey, while other times they wait in the open
like alligators, on top of rocks or in the weeds, motionless and
expertly camouflaged. In either case they're hard to approach.
Only when the ling is sure that it blends in well enough with its
surroundings will it allow a potential enemy to get close. Most
lings will spook as you near, retreating into their rocky redoubts
or swimming away, though occasionally you find a ling that
stands its ground, confident that you can't see it. These are the
lings you want to look for, the confident ones.

Even after you locate a truculent ling, the game has only just
begun. Stealth is paramount. Above all, you cannot reveal your
real intentions—no sudden movements, no clumsy maneuvering.
You approach as if you have no idea the ling is there...dumpty-
dum...looking away, minding your own business, keeping your
swimming strokes to a minimum, careful not to blow an excitable
storm of bubbles. Who knows what the ling sees in you: part foe,
part ungainly curiosity. Often it's best to come up from below,
arms and legs motionless, allowing your natural inclination
toward the surface to carry you forward like a piece of drifting
flotsam, your spear already cocked and pointed forward.

If you can get into shooting range without alarming the ling,
the crucial element is your aim. A headshot is almost always
necessary to bring them to net, and even then it has to be a dead-
on strike. A glancing blow will send the fish into deeper water,
where it will sulk out of sight. Even a good body shot almost
always results in a thrashing battle and the ling shaking off.
(More than once I've seen a healthy ling with a telltale cluster of
three white dots on its side, the scar left from a previous encounter with a spear—probably mine or, more likely, Dave's.) The best
placement is behind the gill plate. If the spear holds, it is essen-
tial to grab hold of the fish immediately—taking care to keep
clear of the gnashing teeth—and ram the points clear through

so the prey can't wriggle off. The smart slinger then gets the fish into his mesh bag, spear and all, before surfacing for air. At the surface the spear tip can be removed while the ling is safely quarantined in the bag. The fish will continue to kick, and often it won't be fully dead until dispatched on shore. I've even had a ling try to take my hand off in the kitchen sink.

On the East Coast lingcod is virtually unknown; on the West Coast it's considered something of a secret delicacy, enjoyed by a confederacy of fish lovers but little known to the general supermarket public. Though it has flaky white flesh reminiscent of cod, the lingcod (*Ophiodon elongatus*) is not a cod at all. A member of the greenling family, it's the only species in its genus. It haunts the Pacific coastline from the Gulf of Alaska to Southern California, dining on a diet of smaller fish, crustaceans, and mollusks. Lings, as anglers usually call them, have large, menacing eyeballs and cigar-chomping lips. Their coloration, though variable, is usually an inconspicuous mottling of brown, gray, and copper. Also known as "bucketheads," they have cavernous mouths filled with razor-sharp canine teeth. Lings don't spawn until at least two years of age, and they're easily susceptible to overfishing. The recreational ling season in Puget Sound has been steadily shrinking in recent years until it's now just a few weeks in May and June. This would be my only ling hunt of the year.

I took another breath and disappeared under for the fifth time. I knew this ling's zip code. Dave already had one in his bag, a thirty-five-incher. The rest of the dive was just swimming for him. Swimming with the fishes. The ling was still in its spot, secure in the belief of its invisibility. I had a clear headshot. With arm and spear outstretched, I glided casually toward the hidey-hole. The ling didn't flinch. At a distance of three feet, I let fly. A flurry of bubbles and the distinct, discouraging sound of metal hitting rock. A missed shot. The ling was gone. I surfaced and examined the spear. Two of the three points were badly dulled. "I think I might have grazed him," I said weakly.

My dive partner submerged without a word and continued along the jetty. Dave's doctoral dissertation was on a concept he referred to as "the inhuman." I've never really understood it, but the theory seemed to be connected to ideas he was having about the natural order of things—about man's need to break free of the mortal coil through art and imagination. The theory also grappled with the notion of human exceptionalism—and the unwillingness of *Homo sapiens* to accept aspects of our own behavior within the context of the nonhuman world. We would be driving around and he'd say look at that: in the gutter would be a road-killed possum. "The inhuman!" he'd howl with obvious delight, going on about how this lowly marsupial lived and died beyond our consciousness, beyond the consciousness of the human-crafted rubber tire that stole its last breath, and yet how its death was so obviously a reminder of our own mortality, how ignoring it dead on the side of the road remained an impossible act. "Act!" he'd say, punctuating the one-syllable word as if it were a bull's-eye for his spear.

Sometimes Dave talked as though every sentence might be his last. The thoughts were carefully worded and expressed with the finality of a eulogy. No clauses petered off to join other half-rendered ideas; each was a self-contained nugget of wisdom from Dave's world. "Four-millimeter is the way you want to go," he said to me firmly not long ago as we rifled through a rack of used wetsuits at a dive shop on Lake Union. "Don't let them talk you into this five-millimeter and six-millimeter bull-*sheeit*. You won't get cold. You're a free diver. You need to get down *unencumbered*." Dave likes the emphasis of italics. He draws out the word with the slight drawl of his mid-Atlantic upbringing and the flattened vowels of a Chesapeake Bay boyhood.

My first spearfishing outing with Dave was off Richmond Beach at Point Wells, north of Seattle. We crossed the railroad tracks in our wetsuits and put on the rest of the gear in the shadow of oil tanks before swimming out to the old derrick where schools of fish circled up out of the deep as if on a spiral staircase. Dave was taken with the surroundings: the somehow lovely interweaving of commercial culture with the wild. White barnacles, purple starfish, and swaying, multicolored bouquets of seaweed decorated the old wooden pilings and rusted rebar. Sometimes broad-shouldered men worked on the platforms above as we swam around below them, and they called down to us to see how we were doing. I practiced my spearing technique on the perch and then moved down the water column in search of bigger prey. Together, that first day, we took a bagful of rock-fish: coppers, quillbacks, even a rare yelloweye. A large cabezon guarded her nest of eggs, and for a moment I thought Dave might spear her too. Back on land, he wielded a serrated buck knife and hummed a Little Walter blues tune as he slit the fish from vent to gill. We cleaned our catch in the surf and fried them up back at Dave's little ranch house on the west slope of Queen Anne hill.

Rockfish were satisfying quarry. They came in all sorts of different colors and sizes and lived in a variety of habitats. They were a challenge to hunt and delicious to eat. But in time we learned other things: rockfish don't spawn until several years old, middle age can be many decades down the road, and old age doesn't come for nearly a century in some species. We were both new to Seattle and just beginning to find our ways around the woods and waterways, learning the names of the plants and animals. This part of the country seemed, at first, far removed from the environmental havoc visited upon our native East Coast states. The rockfish were all around us, there for the taking. But the more we learned, the less we wanted to catch them. Until we stopped altogether.

Lingcod are still on the menu, if only barely. People have hunted lings for at least 5,000 years. Native Americans revered them because, unlike salmon, they could be caught any time of year. White settlers began commercial fishing in earnest in the mid-1800s. Between 1948 and 1967, the total annual Pacific catch, including Canada, was 4,775 tons. By 1984 the commercial lingcod harvest in the United States alone was more than 4,000 tons, mostly through bottom trolling. Lingcod were overfished in Puget Sound, the Georgia Strait, and elsewhere. Populations seem to be recovering with stricter rules, although the recreational fishery is now larger than the commercial.

Dave used to get his share of lings before the season started getting shorter. Now he doesn't hunt rockfish at all and says this might be his last ling hunt in Puget Sound. Since all my spearing has been in his company, I guess it could be my last hunt as well. The lings available to us—that is, those that are within the free diver's rather limited range—are not doing so well. The Sound is ailing, and those lings still hanging on around the urban shore are, according to recent studies, loaded with all sorts of nasty chemicals. No one thought it could happen here—the water looked so scenic from the top deck of a ferry—but pollution and development, coupled with a lack of political will, have taken a toll. Dave wants to have a baby with his wife; today's lingcod, he says again, is his last. This is a hard pill to swallow. He shrugs it off unconvincingly. "I'm a reformed hunter," he says. "The dive is enough. I don't need to hunt."

In Dave's formative waters of Chesapeake Bay, striped bass are filled with so many hormones from fertilizers, pesticides, and pharmaceuticals that it's now common to see hermaphrodites—fish with both male and female reproductive organs. As in male stripers loaded with eggs.

"Well, that's progress, isn't it?" Dave notes bitterly. "Men having babies. The dream is finally realized."

For the next hour we hunted the jetty looking for other lings, but the outgoing tide had likely sent them to deeper water. I was getting chilled. Soon my body would enter the early stages of hypothermia, that punch-drunk state characterized by lack of coordination and sluggishness that is the first indication that the body is shutting down from cold. I had felt it before at the end of a long dive. We still had to cross the boat channel on the other side of jetty and sneak onto a private boat dock. It was time to accept defeat.

Up ahead I could make out the open water we would need to cross. Not seeing bottom always made me nervous. I came to this free diving business rather by accident, to be honest. Soon after moving to the Northwest, I attended one of Dave's memorable crab feeds, and was so knocked out by my first Dungeness crab that I agreed on the spot to join him on his next expedition. The truth is, I was not exactly a water person, and I didn't come from a line of water people. We were landlubbers. In fact, I was one of those impressionable kids profoundly affected by the movie *Jaws* when it first came out in the summer of '75. Rather than vow to never go into the water again, my reaction was to learn as much as I could about these underwater eating machines. And I learned enough to know that the odds of being attacked by a shark are far worse than those of being struck by lightning. But the imagination is a funny thing. The round, black, inscrutable eye of the great white stuck with me. I see that eye out of the corner of my mask whenever I go down. There are no great whites in Puget Sound….Well, maybe—and maybe not. They've been seen feeding on dead whales in the Strait of Juan de Fuca, and not long ago a salmon fisherman reported seeing a shark in the Sound that was bigger than his eighteen-foot boat. Besides, we have orcas. There are no historical records of an orca attack on a human being, but there's always a first, right? The point is, when I go underwater, I take some baggage with me.

These dark thoughts are not rational. Nearby I can hear the barking of sea lion pups. They're hauled out somewhere on the jetty. If there is one dangerous creature in the water, it would be a territorial sea lion. Once during a dive I unknowingly got too close to a group of sea lions. The big male rushed at me with a terrific wake and reared up out of the water. That's a thousand pounds of pissed-off blubber with teeth. I blew bubbles and drank seawater in my eggbeater race to reverse course. Now, as I mentally prepared to cross the channel and go home empty-handed, Dave surfaced behind me and yelled, "Ling!" through his snorkel.

The coldness in my limbs disappeared. I forgot about sharks

and sea lions and orcas. I was a hunter again, and I swam back along the jetty. It was a tough shot, Dave said; the ling was in deep water, but it was out in the open. Generally I didn't go much more than ten or fifteen feet down, rarely twenty. Dave could dive thirty feet with no problem and coast along the bottom for a minute or more. He was laughing now. "We've got a cooperative ling here. What are you waiting for?" Well, for one thing I would need to equalize: I pinched my nose and pushed the air out until my ears filled. This made it possible to go deeper without the resulting pressure headaches. I dove down with my sling uncocked to get a bearing. The fish was right where Dave said it would be. Though it was deep, it wasn't entirely beyond the realm of possibility. I surfaced, cocked my spear, took a breath, and dove again, scissor-kicking vigorously to get down. Silvery perch scattered. At ten feet the water darkened and I eased my kicking. Fifteen feet. Twenty. I was running out of breath. My approach was less than balletic. It was enough just to get down that deep. The fish spooked as I took my shot. A cloud of sediment mushroomed off the bottom. The points missed the head and hit just above the dorsal fin. Even so, we were attached. We thrashed through the water toward the surface, the ling twisting madly in a swirling galaxy of bubbles. Forgetting about the teeth, I tried to grab it by the head and plunge my spear tip, but the fish spun out of my grip and shook off the spear. It dove for deeper water and I watched it go. The three wounds of my spear stuck out like white beacons in the gloom.

At the surface, Dave was asking if I got him. There was no time to explain. I took a breath and went under again. This time I would need to go to my maximum depth. Fifteen feet under, I could see the ling on the sandy bottom, another ten feet below. It was badly wounded. Though my second shot wasn't great—another spinal jab—two of the prongs went to the hilt and I had the ling firmly on my spear. I needed air. Pushing off the bottom with my flippers, I was able to turn the fish and get it above me, then drive it to the surface on the spear. On top I took a breath and then brought the fish into my arms. Into the bag it went, still struggling. Now I could ram the spear points home.

Call it the *Lord of the Flies* impulse. The act of spearing a large fish underwater while holding your breath until bursting is transformative. I called all my friends and invited them over for the feast. Even while its tender fillets sizzled on the barbecue, the ling's severed head—impaled on a spike—kept watch over the outdoor deck where everyone gathered. They laughed outright at the sight and mocked me for my hubris. Their bemusement meant nothing to me. I had ventured into an alien and hostile environment, braved the elements, and returned with snaggle-toothed booty. It was something few had done and not many would attempt. Pride was all around, blaring like a John Philip Sousa march, and for a day at least, I was immune to ridicule.

Dave may say he's giving up spearing, but I don't believe him. Every now and then, we talk about other places. Pristine coves up north in British Columbia. "Maybe one day," he concedes, though for now he's plenty occupied. His wife is pregnant. Soon he'll be a father, and he's got his students and poetry and "scientific" diving: the meticulous logs he keeps of each dive and what he sees and where he sees it. A while back Dave and his wife moved to Kentucky, where there was a good teaching job. He shrugged off the landlocked factor. "I'll be fine," he kept saying. "They've got golf courses down there. I'll dive for golf balls in the water traps, sell 'em on the side. Make some money." He was back within a year.

South of Shilshole, on a hillside that's slowly slipping into the Sound, there's a greenbelt where local kids have an old tire strung up from a stout madrone. It's the sort of dogpatch where street people sometimes weather the rain in ratty sleeping bags and kids drink at night. Chanting "rope swing!" at the top of his lungs like a deranged pied piper, Dave led a group of us there one night after a raucous dinner of ling and chips. Something about a fish fry brings out the Huck Finn in us all. No one was surprised he had ferreted out this secret spot known mostly to teenagers and drunks. It was dark and creepy in the woods. Rainier Beer cans littered the ground. Someone produced a flashlight, and we scoured the bushes for hidden thugs. And then I was climbing up a tree with the tire under my arm and Dave's chanting in the background. I leapt into the void.

The arc of the swing took me well out over the hillside—over a cliff, really—so that I was perhaps fifty or sixty feet off the ground, or so it seemed. A fall was out of the question. Before me, as I emerged from the line of trees, lay the flickering city—the high-rise buildings of downtown, the Space Needle, the bridges over the Ship Canal; and closer, the commercial piers and loading docks; and right below, the upscale boats of a marina clanging gently in the breeze. The whole city by the Sound glimmered beautifully in the night, and its lights warbled in the water's reflection like the visual representation of an echo. From the air it seemed for a moment like the city and the water had merged into one. I careened back into the woods, where someone in the dark gave me another push and I sailed out one more time, spinning wildly, watching the lights dancing below in a blur. Dave's voice carried out across the expanse. *"The inhuman!"*

BEER-BATTERED LING AND CHIPS

Who doesn't like a greasy batch of fish and chips? If you raised your hand, I've got a nice quiche for you in the microwave. Cod is the staple for this classic clam-shack finger food on either side of the Atlantic, though British chippies will also offer haddock and plaice and sometimes hake, monkfish, and even skate; halibut is the top-drawer offering on the American West Coast. Why lingcod rarely appears as a fish-and-chip contender is something of a mystery, since it's richer than cod and nearly as flaky as halibut, not to mention much cheaper. Such nose-thumbing shouldn't stop the enterprising spearfisher or angler who wants first-rate deep-fried fish.

1 beer (12 ounces)
1 egg, beaten
1½ cups flour
2 teaspoons fresh lemon zest
½ teaspoon paprika
½ teaspoon cayenne pepper
1 teaspoon salt
½ teaspoon black pepper
2 pounds lingcod fillets, sliced into 5-inch chunks
Vegetable oil for frying

Make batter by combining beer, egg, flour, lemon zest, and seasonings. Dredge lingcod pieces in batter, gently shaking off any excess; put aside battered pieces on a plate. Pour enough oil into a deep pan so that it comes up the pan sides at least one inch. Heat on medium-high, being careful not to let oil smoke or boil; you don't want the batter to cook before the fish. When a small splash of water on the oil pops and sizzles, it's ready. Place battered fish carefully in the oil with tongs. Cook until golden; with the correct oil temperature, this should take about 2 minutes per side. Remove fish to paper towels or newspaper to draw off any extra oil.

Eat with french fries, coleslaw, and Cajun tartar sauce. And beer, of course. WITH SIDE DISHES, SERVES 4

SHAD DARTS AT DAWN

BEEDLE'S BEEN WATCHING fish counts at the ladder. Though the salmon and steelhead runs have mostly gone kittywampus, other options swim upstream. Throughout May the numbers trend up until, late in the month, there's a big spike. "Time to hit the river!" he barks at me over the phone. Martha can hear his voice blasting through the receiver clear on the other side of the kitchen. She shakes her head, knowing I'm about to abandon her once again to go fishing.

Foraging at the dawn of the twenty-first century is a weird mix of opportunity and regret. On the one hand, you can go just about anywhere with a decent road map and a sense of adventure. On the other, these places reveal glimpses into a long-gone past that was surely a forager's paradise. If you squint at sixty miles per hour on the Columbia River Highway, you can almost see the ghost of the once-treacherous gorge that greeted Lewis and Clark in 1805, and the once-powerful, salmon-choked river flowing through it.

Almost.

At any rate, the same cascades still plummet over cliffs high above the road: Latourell, Bridal Veil, Wahkeena. The sight of Multnomah Falls makes Beedle crack a smile. "Some McGrue hiked all the way up there with a few boxes of Tide," he says, looking at me expectantly. Did I get it? Beedle has a way, when he's telling a story, of making his face do all the work—he's got bulging eyes and a bald pate with a few tufts of salt-and-pepper hair behind each ear. "The place was a bubble bath!" he shouts finally. This makes him laugh, and laugh some more.

McGrue. Beedle has a way with language; his is a cross between the scientific and the Seussian. He claims that every word in his vocabulary has a dictionary definition, but I'm not so sure. This time around I've remembered to carry a little notebook and pen so I can get the correct spellings and check for myself. It doesn't take long before the pad comes out. We pass a group of sign-holders on the roadside, adherents to some sort of political philosophy that Beedle finds morally repugnant. "Look at all of them," he laughs. "Like spalled-off pieces of exfoliated scree." He glances over at me, at the pad. "That's *spalled*—s-p-a-double-l-e-d. There you go. Spalled off. Fragments of old rock. That's a geologic term. I wouldn't expect you to know it. Dinosaurs, that's what they are, living in the past."

The past and the present are forever at odds in Beedle's world. If only he could take the best from each and mash them together. Like cars, for instance. He loves the freedom of the open road but hates what cars are doing to the environment, and he detests other drivers even more. One of the many inventions Beedle threatens to patent is a video monitor for the back of a car that would be operated from the dashboard—a way to communicate with other drivers without honking horns and raising middle digits. For safety's sake, certain common messages would be kept in memory, like radio stations, so you could push a single key and the message would scroll across the back: "Nice turn signal, lady!" Or "Back off, Butthook!"

We come up behind a lumbering RV—a "land whale"—with a caricature of a coonskin-capped Davy Crockett on the back, and Beedle starts to fume. The RV culture is exactly what's wrong with America, he says. In protest, Beedle clings to a modicum of self-sufficiency—heating his house, for instance, with firewood that he bucks up and splits himself. The other thing about Beedle is that he needs to have quantities of fish on hand at all times. He grew up fishing the Nestucca, Neskowin, and other coastal rivers for salmon. He remembers hauling in summer steelhead as a kid on Oregon's Rogue River in the '60s. "You could go down to the river just about any evening in August and catch a fish half as big as yourself." The dams and hatcheries have changed all that. The fish are smaller—mostly half-pounders and hatchery stock now—and they come back later, if at all.

Beedle still gets some salmon in the fall, but when he really wants to stock his larder he turns elsewhere, taking along his usual flyrod and a pair of pants that are his designated fishing gear. The rod is an ancient Sage and the pants are permanent press of unknown source, with a crease down each leg that's so knife-edged, even after all these years, that the pant material has rubbed off in the wash, revealing a pinstripe of dark liner underneath. Beedle prefers them this way. When it rains, he pulls on a rubber yellow slicker of the sort worn by the Morton Salt girl. You won't find Beedle in Gore-Tex or any other trendy, high-tech clothing. Taught to hunt and fish and build useful things like shake cabins by an itinerant gold miner from the Rogue River country named Red Keller, Beedle approaches the sporting life from the turn of the previous century.

At Bonneville Dam we exit the highway and get in line for the 7:00 AM starting gun. The insult of this queue is almost too much for Beedle, on a par with taking off your boots at the airport because of some half-wit shoe bomber. "You know," he muses, "it used to be you could park here from 5:00 AM till 10:00 PM, and you didn't need to have your testicles examined by Homeland Security." Several other beat-up cars are ahead of us in line, everyone here to catch and kill a mess of fish. It's June and the shad run is on.

The American shad is silver, with a bluish-green back, a few dark spots across the shoulder, and a forked tail. In the right light, though, it can flash all the colors in the rainbow, with large round scales that milk the sun like a disco ball. Its mouth is slightly upturned and soft. If the shad looks like an oversized herring, that's because it is. At one to eight pounds, it's the largest member of the herring family, *Clupeidae*, differing mainly from its exclusively saltwater cousins in its anadromy and deeper belly.

American shad return to their natal rivers to spawn after three to five years at sea. The female, larger than the male and carrying up to 600,000 eggs, extrudes her eggs in open water, where they're fertilized by the male before settling on the bottom. Larvae hatch out in twelve to fifteen days and then drift downstream with the current before growing into juveniles that resemble their parents. In fall the young shad leave the river for salt water. Unlike salmon, shad can survive the rigors of reproduction to spawn again.

John McPhee calls the American shad the Founding Fish because of its economic importance to the first colonists. In the winter and spring of 1777–78, General Washington fortified his weary, malnourished troops with smoked shad at Valley Forge after a good run on the Delaware and Schuylkill rivers, possibly altering the outcome of the Revolutionary War. And during the Civil War shad supposedly played a supporting role in Confederate troop desertions as enlistments returned to their traditional fishing weirs during the shad runs. Its scientific name, *Alosa sapidissima*, means "most delicious."

On the East Coast, fresh-cooked shad is a staple in many mid-Atlantic homes in spring, when the snowy white blossoms of serviceberry, also known as shadbush, announce the fish's arrival. The shad's flesh, though shot through with little bones, is firm and white, with a sweet, pleasing flavor unlike any other fish; its roe, tightly encased in two reddish-orange sacs, is considered a delicacy. In *The Boston Cooking-School Cook Book* (1896), Fannie Farmer recommends boiling the shad roe for fifteen minutes with half a teaspoon of vinegar and then baking it in tomato sauce. The lowcountry cooks of South Carolina like to top their grits with fried roe and bacon. Many recipes get around the bone issue by calling for pulverized shad in croquettes or by slow-baking the fish until its bones dissolve. And while Northwesterners might consider themselves owners of the cedar-plank method of barbecuing salmon, shad have been broiled on a plank over an open fire since at least 1732, as documented by a Philadelphia fishing club. Throughout its culinary history there have been plenty of doubters and naysayers, too. One joke goes like this: "Put shad on board, place in smoker, when done toss shad and eat board."

On the West Coast, shad aren't native but they're here to stay, which is more than you can say about salmon and steelhead some years. They were first introduced in 1871, when pioneering aquaculturist Seth Green, just off a weeklong trip by train only two years after completion of the transcontinental railway, planted 10,000 newly hatched Hudson River shad fry in California's Sacramento River. By the time Frederick Jackson Turner announced the closing of the American frontier, in 1890, shad had spread as far north as Alaska. The year of Bonneville Dam's completion, 1938, only some 5,000 shad entered the Columbia. The population exploded with completion of The Dalles Dam, in 1956, and the inundation of Celilo Falls; shad could now move up into the Snake River. This year's run was predicted to be a few million.

The Washington State Department of Fish and Wildlife calls shad the lottery fish: *When you're talking shad, you're talking big numbers. But there's one major difference—shad are a lot easier to come by than those million-dollar lottery payoffs. Hit the Columbia River below Bonneville Dam from late May through June and you're likely to hook into a million-count shad jackpot.*

That was the plan. I had bought my ticket and here I was, right below one of the biggest hydro projects in the world. Bonneville doesn't win points for scenery—unless massive, Depression-era engineering feats turn your crank—but for pure foraging value there are far worse places to fill the freezer. For one thing, every anadromous fish that plans to fulfill its mating urge upstream will need to take a number at the fish ladder, which means traffic jams and pileups right where the fishermen congregate. For another, it's a short drive from Beedle's house in Portland, underscoring an inescapable fact: modern-day hunter-gatherers are just as likely to live in large metropolitan areas as in the more traditional rural parts.

Cars continue to rattle in and park at the back of the line. Like the country at large, the diverse ranks of anglers form less a melting pot than an á la carte steamer tray, with a lot of variety and all of it compartmentalized. Because Beedle has seen some ugly incidents between the white and Asian anglers, he was surprised the other day when a Cambodian man came over to watch his fly-fishing technique. Beedle didn't see him at first, so when the man yelled "Fish on!" Beedle nearly jumped off his rock into the river. His one-man cheering section stayed to watch him catch another four fish before heading back to his party, but not before declaring, "You number one."

It's true, he has to admit, he is something of a master with the flyrod. "Watch and learn," he instructs me. For years Beedle taught high school science, and it shows. He's one of those born teachers you sometimes meet who's forever passing along his knowledge on a variety of subjects to those who will listen. He's taught me any number of things, from the finer points of cribbage to how to repair a ruptured water main. Sometimes he can get caught up in the details. If you need driving directions, Beedle will gladly draw you detailed maps and diagrams. Need to get from point A to point B? He's only too happy to help. But did you know that point C and point D are actually on the way, if you take the back route? You should see those. And here, here's a map showing each light signal, each bend in the road and convenience store. Get your gas here—you'll save at least five cents on the gallon. In his tiny script he'll jot down the distances in tenths of a mile. It's not quite to scale, but you get the idea.

We open the hatch and inventory our stuff. Apropos of nothing, the man behind us boasts about his Honda ("300,000 miles—without a rebuild, mind you") and admires our gear. "I did that as a younger man," he says, craning his neck out the window. "Fished for steelhead all up and down this river with a fly."

"Why'd you quit?" Beedle asks.

"It's a younger man's sport. Besides, ain't no steelhead left."

Beedle looks around. "Well, I don't know, I've been fishing with a flyrod for half a century and I'm not ready to put it down yet."

"Just you wait," says the man.

"You're probably right about the steelhead. But these shad are thick, and they like flies."

"Just you wait," says the man again.

Then the first engines start up and it's time to check in with the dam parking guards. "Just you wait?" says Beedle back in the cab, his face all knotted up. "Wait for what?" He jams the truck into first gear. Beedle has had two major back surgeries, including a spinal fusion, and if anything, he feels better today than a decade ago.

"Maybe he didn't mean it personally," I offer. "Maybe he was speaking in more general, apocalyptic terms."

Two uniformed officers lean in and ask to see the back of the truck. Since 9/11, Bonneville Dam has been regarded as a temptation to terrorists, a security risk. "Good luck," one of the guards says a moment later. Beedle punches the gas and we drive across the boat locks and past the powerhouse to Bradford Island, where we park below the spillway and walk down a steep trail to the river.

The Columbia River has nothing to do with Christopher Columbus, contrary to the beliefs of some. The river was named by Captain Robert Gray, an American born in Rhode Island who sailed his ship, the *Columbia Rediviva*, into its estuary in 1792 while exploring the local fur trade. The Columbia is the largest river by volume that flows into the Pacific, and at one time it was thought to be a leg of the fabled Northwest Passage through the continent.

What Beedle doesn't know is that I already have some history with the river. The first time I saw the Columbia, I was crossing the Hood River Bridge from Oregon to White Salmon, Washington, where, during a summer break from college, I had arranged to rent a puke-green shack smothered by brambles on the north bank for a couple of months. The rent was something like $50 for one of the bedrooms plus use of a communal hot plate. A friend and I took turns sleeping on the only available mattress while the other slept on a couch. We had traveled all the way from Vermont to harness the wind.

In its northern headwaters, the Columbia drains a big chunk of southern British Columbia, eastern Washington, and western Montana. In most of Washington it flows through what might be best described as high desert scablands—hot, dry places where constant floods of biblical proportion across the ages have dug up the earth's crust and thrown it around like so much potting soil. This is canyon country, home to hawks and rattlesnakes, a land of high blue skies in summer. The Northwest coast, on the other hand, is a place where it can feel like winter in August. Clouds pile up off the Pacific, and fogbanks drop in for long, uninvited visits. Meanwhile, the Columbia acts as a conduit: high pressure, meet low pressure. The result is a sailboarder's paradise, with nearly constant winds sucked through the river gorge. Though my mind was mostly on learning to short-board that summer, it was impossible not to notice the flotillas of fishermen tucked into bays and tributary mouths along the river. I was eating bologna sandwiches for breakfast, lunch, and dinner, and these guys were packing home coolers full of fresh fish fillets. Somehow I knew I'd be back again, with a hunger.

Below the dam, the bank is shored up with riprap. Wearing our felt-soled boots for better purchase, we pick our way out onto the rocks like crabs at low tide. In an environment such as this one, it's easy to feel puny and insubstantial. Water and sky arm-wrestle for bragging rights. The day is overcast with a slight wind blowing downstream. Fog shrouds the hills on the Washington side, and occasional gusts carry a fine mist that dampens our faces. Basalt cliffs stare out of the spring-green gorge like red eyes. To the east we can see the mountains where the Pacific Crest Trail winds down through the Columbia wilderness to its crossing over the Bridge of the Gods. Foam floats and tumbles in the current, sometimes taking to the air like embers from a fire. The last of the windblown cottonwood seeds drifts past on the breeze. Upstream the river boils and roars in outrage. The sound of its fury overshadows everything else. We stand in the lee of the first of twelve dams that subdue the once mighty Columbia. Even yoked and defanged, the river still feels huge.

What can be said about this river that hasn't already been said? I try to put myself in a dugout canoe, circa 1805, but the wires keep getting in the way. Power lines from the dam cross the river to large orange-and-white towers on the north side. Other guy wires, strewn with errant wreaths of nylon filament and lead weights, run helter-skelter overhead. The scene reminds me of an illustrated edition of *Gulliver's Travels* from my childhood, of how the picture of Gulliver tied down by the Lilliputians always struck me as unlikely. *Just get up and flex your strength.* To my eye, this binding matrix of electricity has a tacked-on and temporary feel to it. In arguing that four dams farther upstream on the Snake River should not be breached to aid ailing fish populations, the Bush White House called the Columbia Basin dams an "immutable" part of the landscape—as if the landscape itself is not dynamic, is not in constant flux—as if concrete and steel can withstand the tectonic teeth-grinding of geologic time.

Slate green water surges past. On the face of it, the idea of fly-fishing the Columbia from shore seems patently absurd. More than a mile across in places, with crashing swells and whitecaps in the wind and devilish currents despite the dams, the river appears to pose the same challenges to an angler as the open ocean. Luckily for us, the shad don't stray far from the banks. I have my six-weight rod, Beedle a seven-weight. We're using heavy sink-tip lines. Beedle produces an Altoids box filled with multicolored shad flies that he tied the night before. The flies, colloquially known as darts, are heavily weighted and bullet-shaped, mostly tied with red or pink thread, and with tufts of yellow or white calf's hair for tails. He's named them after the so-called advisory system managed by the Department of Homeland Security, the color-coded alerts used to monitor terrorist threat levels.

"Grab a handful of these," Beedle says. "Let's see, we've got all different threat levels. Here's a Yellow Elevated, that's a good one. This is Orange High."

"I'll take a bunch of the Red Severes."

"Here you go. Now tie one on and then run a dropper line off your leader like this"—he demonstrates with a fifteen-inch section of six-pound test—"and there, you have a diddle on the dangle."

Fly-fishing for shad can be tiring at the height of the run, what with the nearly constant action, and when the shad are on the bite you know right away. Which is why we're nervous after an hour of futile casting. "No sun," Beedle declares. He's convinced that the shad become more active in sunlight, pointing to fish counts over the dam, the high tallies of which correlate with sunny weather, as empirical evidence in support of his theory. This theory flies in the face of almost everything you hear, but I tend to side with Beedle.

A moment later his rod is doubled over, and a moment after that, so is mine. Shad are funny that way. Hookups often come in pairs, or even threes and fours, as if the fish are synchronized. "That's schooling fish for you," Beedle says. "Class is in session!" On a flyrod they usually hit at the end of the drift, so you're fighting a four-pound fish that's downstream in strong current. Twin barbed hooks make up for this disadvantage. Unlike a species that might have to be thrown back—a steelhead or salmon that turns out to be from an endangered wild stock—all these shad will go on the stringer, so barbless hooks are strictly voluntary. In a throwback to days gone by, there are no limits in Columbia River shad fishing.

As a fighting fish, shad earn a solid B. Only the largest females are capable of taking much line off your reel. Still, even a small male puts up a good enough resistance in its own way. It might try to go deep and get behind a rock, or thrash around on the surface. Rarely does one get airborne. Once near the bank I use the current swells to pull the fish in on the rocks and then hoist it up to my perch, where I dispatch it with a rock to the head and thread a rope through its mouth and gill. Killing fish is a bloody business. I don't like to do it, but if you're going to eat something, you might as well be the one doing the killing.

For the next two hours the shad fishing is hot—at least for those of us with flyrods, which is probably a total of two on both sides of the river. The legions of spincasters pull in the occasional shad while Beedle and I hook up with fish after fish, often simultaneously. Our piles of shad get larger. I can't explain why this is so, except to speculate that the shad like something about the movement of a dead-drifted dart through the water, an action that's hard to duplicate without a flyrod and heavy line. We're feeling pretty good about our haul. I hook a big one that skitters through the swells before washing up on the rocks. "You number one," Beedle yells over to me. Just before lunch a fish grabs my dart and takes off downstream, ripping line off the reel until it throws the hook fifty yards out. Beedle sees it too. We look at each other from across the rocks. "You never know," he says. "Could have been a summer steelhead."

"Yeah," I agree. "Could have been."

Around noon a gear fisherman walks by, decked out in a camo jacket with a big burlap sack over his shoulder, and sets up just downstream of us. His hair is matted, as if he's just woken up, and we can see his five o'clock shadow from a hundred paces. He wears wraparound mirror sunglasses. Beedle and I grin at each other as if to say, "Get a load of this guy!" He might have been sleeping under a bridge. As we eat our tortillas rolled with canned shad salad from last year's catch, the gear guy gets his rig together and then starts catching fish left and right, with hardly a letup. "Old Burlap knows what he's doing," Beedle concedes.

Soon he's got more than either of us. "You must like shad an awful lot," I call over to him.

Burlap shakes his head. "Not so much anymore. This is sturgeon bait. I'm a professional sturgeon guide." Sturgeon are primitive bottom-feeders. They mostly cruise the substrate, using catfish-like feelers called barbels to identify food. Then they vacuum up whatever they can get in their mouths. He explains the process, how the sturgeon move upriver during the shad run, partly to feed on the dead and injured shad, partly because their spawning grounds are up here. Whole shad are used with stout poles to hook them. The big ones—longer than sixty inches—are called oversized because they exceed the keeper limit. They're also known as peelers for their tendency to peel line off a reel. "It's like hooking into a train," Burlap says. These oversized peeler sturgeon have a third name: poor man's marlin. A hooked peeler will usually jump at least once, a prehistoric, armor-plated monster leaping from the depths to thrill its antagonists.

"But these goddamn sea lions," he grumbles, and drifts off in painful reverie. His livelihood is in jeopardy due to the sea lions that swim 150 miles up the Columbia from the ocean to feast on what's left of the salmon and steelhead stacked up at the fish ladder. "The goddamn bastards have eaten up all the salmon, and now they're going after sturgeon. Hard to believe, but I've seen it. A few hundred pounds of fish, and they take a plug right out of the belly. They've got actual pictures of sea lions taking down a peeler sturgeon." He pauses to let the gravity of this situation sink in. Some of those sturgeon on the bottom of the river might have been swimming around when Lewis and Clark came down. "They're a hundred, two hundred years old. Who knows? Seen a lot of bullshit, that's for sure. Now chewed up by a goddamn sea

lion. It's not right." He says biologists found an eighteen-footer.
"Mouth like a fifty-five-gallon drum. Scared the diver. He didn't
want to be swimming with no eighteen-foot sturgeon." It's not
all that hard, in this oversized environment, to imagine a sucker
bigger than a great white shark somewhere out there, skulking
around down at the foot of the dam.

Burlap smiles. "The old-timers knew how to deal with the
sea lions," he says, and stalks away like a hunchback, his catch
over his shoulder. I know better than to argue with him. Sea
lions are an emotional issue. Still, it's not their fault. You almost
have to credit the sea lions with learning how to exploit the fish
ladders. But he'll probably put a slug in one anyway, if given a
chance, and you can't really blame him either.

"That's one tough hombre," Beedle says with admiration. I
tell him about a sturgeon-fishing brochure I've seen: *You had better bring your Gatorade and Bengay because these fish will work you
like a job! These fish will break rods, smoke reels, and leave you standing there with a "what in the hell just took 300 yards of line and never
even slowed down" look on your face!*

"Good action," says Beedle in approval.

It's time to pack it in. Beedle uses a pair of heavy scissors to open
up the females and retrieve their egg skeins. One of his favorite
meals is shad roe floured and fried with eggs in a lot of butter.
The deep red skeins cook up brown like sausages, and their taste
is one of the richest and meatiest I've found anywhere. Poached in
boiling water with a dash of vinegar, they keep in the freezer for a
year. The fried roe is almost too much for me, although I indulge
in it with Beedle, who enjoys nothing more than "whumping up"
huge meat-and-potato meals with his catch of the day. My own
plans involve filleting several shad for my smoker at home. The
year before, I discovered that a cup of pineapple juice added to
the standard brine of pickling salt, brown sugar, and water gives
the smoked fillets a light tropical flavor that's irresistible. I take
a knife to the shad and remove the scales that give them such

a beautiful rainbow hue. The scales come off easily in clumps, sticking to my hands and arms. Back at Beedle's house, with a garden hose running, I'll finish the smelly business of filleting the fish. But first, we have a stop to make.

In Oregon City, at the end of the Oregon Trail and just around the corner from the covered wagons of the End of the Oregon Trail Interpretive Center, is a flashback to earlier days when the rivers of the Northwest teemed with fish. Tony's Smokehouse & Cannery is a ramshackle collection of tin-roof sheds and storefront at the corner of Fourteenth and Washington Streets. Rows of cans decorate one wall: smoked albacore tuna, smoked salmon, smoked sturgeon, even smoked Dungeness crab. This is Tony's stock-in-trade. Besides buying Tony's canned goods, you can bring in your own catch and have it cleaned, smoked, and pressure-canned. There's also plenty of gape-mouthed fish on ice. A hand-scrawled poster on the wall says, "Ask me about Ami's coffee buzz," but a young clerk in an apron says the joe is no more special than that from anywhere else. I guess they don't need to plug the coffee because they're already selling enough fish. At $2.10 per can to smoke and can our shad—fish that we caught and delivered—somebody's making money. Just the same, it's a small price to pay to have someone else deal with all those little bones.

There's no denying that shad are bony in the extreme. A Lenape Indian legend has it that a porcupine, unhappy with his lot in life, asked the Great Spirit for a change; the Great Spirit turned him inside out and threw him in the river. Shad have double layers of Y-shaped ribs that resist easy filleting. Most people don't even bother trying to remove all the bones, figuring they'll come out more easily once cooked. Tony's circumvents the bone issue altogether by applying such heat and compression that the bones are rendered soft. The resulting canned shad has a consistency like tuna, and it makes a terrific sandwich. Beedle still has a box of canned shad in his basement from the year before. "You never know when you might need thirty cans of shad," he says.

It's past three by the time we get out of Tony's and already the afternoon commute is grinding the roads to a halt. Normally this sort of traffic would have Beedle red-faced and apoplectic, but we've been fishing and catching all day—and will soon be eating our day's work—so Beedle is feeling more generous toward his fellow commuters. "Nice move," he says brightly to an SUV that suddenly changes lanes in front of us. "You know, studies have proved that changing lanes doesn't get you anywhere any faster"—here he lurches into an opening in the right lane—"but it sure does make you feel better."

"Ever wish you could go back to the days of the horse-and-buggy?" I ask Beedle.

"Goes without saying. More salmon in the rivers."

"Just you wait."

"When we blow this whole thing up, the salmon will be back to reclaim their home from the shad. They're resilient critters."

We pass the spot of an accident from the day before, a semi that jackknifed, tying up I-5 for miles. Bad portents are everywhere. Beedle is momentarily animated, recalling the chaos. "You wouldn't believe what a mess it was," he says. "Machinery and humanity tangled up all over the road. The guy bounced off the median in one of those big rigs and came to rest slaunchwise across the highway, blocking all southbound lanes. All of 'em."

Slaunchwise?

"That's right, he was slaunched across the highway. You know, slaunchwise. Hey, what have you got there?"

Beedle tries to read over my shoulder as he shifts gears. I close my notebook. "Just jotting down a few things before I forget. Local color and that sort of thing. Slaunchwise."

"Get that down. That's a word you need to know. And *diddle*, did you get that?"

Back at the house we fillet the rest of the shad. It feels good to have a cooler filled with fresh fish and know that a box of canned shad is in my future. True, it would feel even better to have a load of salmon, but we can't complain. Beedle has recently sold his tutoring business, and though he tries to be optimistic, now that he's in his mid-fifties it isn't likely he can go back to his original career, teaching high school biology. The summer is often a time of rest for educators, though this summer I expect will offer more uncertainty than rest for my friend. As I back out of his driveway I ask him what he's up to for the dry months. For a moment he looks totally serene, without a care in the world. "Driving school," he barks at me finally. "I'll teach the kiddies to drive. How about that!"

WHOLE SHAD, COOKED LOW & SLOW, CAROLINA STYLE

Deboning shad is a chore left to sinners in fishmonger hell. The low-country cooks of coastal South Carolina approach shad like a hunk of pork shoulder: they do it low and slow, until the bones are mostly dissolved or rendered soft. This recipe comes from fellow forager and proprietor of the Hunter Angler Gardener Cook blog, Hank Shaw, who did time on both a fishing boat and a reporter's beat in mid-Atlantic shad country.

Shad is meaty and flavorful in a way that's surprising for fish, so serve with mashed potatoes and a solid Chardonnay. If you have a female fish and saved the roe like any true shad lover, poach the egg skeins briefly with a dash of vinegar and a pinch of salt, then fry in butter. They brown up nicely like sausages. Serve with eggs and toast for breakfast, or with mashed potatoes and onion gravy for dinner—an American version of bangers and mash.

> 2 tablespoons salt
> 1 tablespoon cider vinegar
> 3 tablespoons Old Bay seasoning
> 1 large whole shad (4 pounds), scaled and gutted
> 3 yellow onions, cut into half-moons
> Freshly ground black pepper to taste
> Smoked bacon to cover fish

In a pan wide enough to fit the shad, boil enough water to cover fish and add 1 tablespoon of the salt, the vinegar, 2 tablespoons of the Old Bay seasoning, and a few grindings of pepper. Add shad to boil, cover, and turn off heat. Let shad steep for 20 minutes.

In an ovenproof dish that is also large enough to hold the shad, add the onions, sprinkle the rest of the salt and Old Bay seasoning over them, and then pour in enough water just to cover the bottom. Place the shad so that it rests on the onions; make sure the shad does not sit in the water. Cover the pan and put it in a 200-degree oven for 4½ hours. After the second, third, and fourth hours, check to see that there is still water in the pan.

After 4½ hours, uncover, lay the bacon over the shad, and broil until the bacon is crispy, a few minutes. SERVES 4

DANDY TIME

I REMEMBER THE moment I went crazy for what the French call *dent de lion,* or lion's tooth. I was standing in an urban jungle in downtown Seattle, where the Dearborn Street on-ramp clover-leafs into I-5. A hummock of green space had been passed over in the highway engineering and was now left to homeless vaga-bonds and dandelions. I was there for the weeds. My car stood alone on a nearby street littered by small piles of broken window glass every few spaces. Sleeping bags and shopping carts lined the sidewalk beneath the overpass. Commuters stuck in morn-ing traffic crawled by. The morning sun was just rising over more affluent neighborhoods to the east, places where the lawns were trimmed and tidy and totally useless for my purposes.

I started to work. My timing was good. The dandelions were still closed up, their petals packed together in tight, vertical clusters. In an hour they would be open to the sun and harder to harvest. A simple twist-and-pull motion with thumb and forefinger was all that was needed to separate the tiny yellow petals from the rest of the green flower head. I started to fill my grocery produce bag, but only a few minutes had gone by before a pair of unofficial residents spotted my suspicious activity from street level and started toward my position on the hill, mov-ing deliberately, like wolves after prey. They stepped through a hole in the chain-link fence and scrambled up a guerrilla path through the undergrowth. *Uh-oh.* I held tightly to my bag, trying to look normal.

"What have you got there?" asked the taller one. He was dressed in a threadworn black trench coat and high-tops. His eyes were seriously bloodshot. We all stared at the bag I was holding. It was plastic and transparent, a cupful of bright yellow petals clearly visible inside.

Looking back up at my interlocutor, at a loss for words, I was reminded of a story about a well-known forager in New York, "Wildman" Steve Brill, who was arrested for picking dandelions in Central Park. It occurred to me that an officer of the law might not be such a bad thing right about now.

The shorter one broke the silence. "I believe he's got dandy lion flowers in the bag." He might have been the muscle. Despite cool spring temps, he was clad in a dirty white Mickey Mouse t-shirt. His biceps bulged out of cut-off sleeves. I tried to smile.

"He's picking dandy lions?" the tall, bleary one questioned his short, stout friend. "This one *es loco.*"

That was the moment I knew for sure I'd gone around the bend. Why was I in such a rundown part of town to begin with? The answer was simple enough: the dandelions in this mostly forgotten blight, unmolested by lawn mowers, herbicides, or other armaments of civilization, were stunningly big and too tempting to pass up. I'd spied them while getting on the highway the day before.

"Why you picking our dandy lions?"

There it was: the claim of ownership. With as casual a tone as I could muster, as if this were an everyday occurrence, I explained that my motivation was harmless: I planned to eat these dandelion petals.

"Those yellow flowers?"

"That's right," I said, getting a little bolder. "I might bake something with them. Bread. Muffins. Maybe cookies." This was the short answer. It seemed beside the point to tell these gentlemen that I was in the process of teaching myself how to bake, that these dandelions—colorful, nutritious, and free—were goading me on to new levels of sophistication in the kitchen. But baking, I was quickly learning, was about as closely related to cooking as robins are to *T. rex*. Yes, there's a connection, but it could seem awfully tenuous at times. For one thing, I was discovering the persnickety side of baking: all those exact measurements, not to mention the adjustments needed for humidity, elevation, even barometer. The adjustment needed for humility. As someone who appreciates the improvisational brio of bebop jazz, this careful attention to detail felt more like practicing the exact notes of a classical sonata for a fanatical instructor. You *will* hit every note.

"Dandy lion cookies?" The men looked hard at me.

"You loco, boy."

Maybe baked goods were the wrong approach. "I could also make dandelion wine," I told them.

The men straightened up in unison.

"Make dandy lion wine with those yellow flowers?"

"I'd need to pick a lot more."

"Like how much?"

"Maybe a couple quarts."

They started looking around. Dandelions were blooming all over the lot, a sea of big yellow Cheshire cat faces staring up at us out of unkempt grass, from underneath a soiled mattress, between beer cans, even up through the peephole of an abandoned pair of navy blue jockey shorts. Silently the two men considered the possibilities.

"That's a day's work," the tall one finally concluded. They frowned and lurched off into the jungle.

I'm not a big fan of the American lawn, that one-note symphony of righteousness that seems to suggest moral rectitude on the part of the homeowner willing to commit himself to a never-ending battle with weeds. As a place to play catch and kick a soccer ball, I'll let you have your backyard turf. But that front lawn of manicured green running from door to sidewalk? That monochromatic parcel of mindless geometry? That Victorian notion of the garden as anchor to the wind of godless wilderness? It needs to go.

My neighbors are forever grappling with the weeds that so easily outwit them at every turn. They pull and mow and dump gallons of fertilizers and herbicides, heedless of the ever-dwindling salmon that will end up drinking in the polluted runoff. Has none of them read *Silent Spring*? Meanwhile, I've let my own lawn go to hell, earning the hairy eyeball as property values around me take the hit. One day I'll rip out the lawn altogether and replace its humdrum bed of grass with a more visually stimulating rock garden of some sort, with native plants that don't require constant coddling like spoiled children. In the interim I'll make use of the lawn's best feature: its dandelions.

For millennia the common dandelion has been revered for its medicinal qualities. In 1753 Linnaeus gave it the scientific name *Leontodon taraxacum*, roughly translated as "medicinal lion's tooth," and in 1779 George Heinrich Weber renamed it *Taraxacum officinale*, or "official remedy." The sick ate its roots in winter and its tender leaves in spring and were restored to health. Now we have vitamin supplements, and the once mighty dandelion has been consigned to a long list of pests to be stamped out. It's too bad. Study after study shows that vitamins absorbed through food are far more effective than any supplement. Dandelions, it turns out, are bursting with vitamins and trace minerals, in part because of those exasperating taproots— the bane of lawn-care professionals everywhere—that can reach two feet or more down into the soil. According to Dr. Peter Gail, president of Defenders of Dandelions, these common weeds "contain more beta-carotene than carrots, more potassium than bananas, more lecithin than soybeans, more iron than spinach, and loads of Vitamins A, C, E, thiamine and riboflavin, calcium, phosphorus, and magnesium."

And they taste good. Gail has written an entire book on the hated weed, *The Dandelion Celebration*, with a decidedly open-minded viewpoint. He includes scores of recipes, many of them submitted by dandelion connoisseurs from coast to coast, some of them quite surprising. After being roasted, for instance, dandelion roots can be ground up to make a coffeelike beverage or used to flavor ice cream. The early spring leaves can add zest to salads, just like any expensive baby lettuce with a French name. They can also be steamed and sautéed like kale or spinach, or cooked with a chunk of salt pork like collards. Europeans regularly cook with dandelion greens. Once the buds appear the leaves become too bitter for most palates, but the buds themselves are a bright addition to omelets (Martha says eating them is like nibbling on a little piece of sunshine), and the flower petals can be used in all sorts of ways, from baking to mead-brewing.

One of my favorite ways to use dandelions is in bread. The yellow petals give the loaf a sunny countenance that belies the simplicity of the recipe, but the real proof of edibility came not long ago when I brought a loaf to a barbecue and watched the amazed faces of a few parents as their kids bypassed platters of corn syrup–infused hotdog rolls and hamburger buns in favor of a dandy treat.

I guess one of these afternoons when the sun is out I'll resuscitate my ancient lawn mower and make my neighbors happy. But first I've got some dandelions to harvest. Call me crazy.

DANDY BREAD AND MUFFINS

This recipe is adapted from one in Peter Gail's The Dandelion Celebration, *the main difference being that I like to double the amount of dandelion petals, for both look and flavor. You can also experiment by adding in different combinations of fresh herbs. Before making this recipe, you'll need to harvest at least a cup of dandelion petals. This shouldn't take more than 20 minutes or so with the right flowers and technique. Choose tall, robust dandelions that have been allowed to grow freely. Abandoned lots and field margins are good places to look. The presence of dandelions usually indicates that herbicides are not in use, but roadside specimens can contain the residue of other chemicals. Choose your spots wisely. You'll want to harvest in the morning, before the flowers have fully opened. Grasp the yellow part of the flower (the petals) and twist away from the green sepals and stem. Discard any greenery.*

2 cups unbleached flour
2 teaspoons baking powder
½ teaspoon salt
1 cup dandelion petals
Scant 1½ cups milk
4 tablespoons honey
¼ cup canola oil
1 egg

In a large bowl combine dry ingredients, including petals, and mix. Make sure to separate any clumps of petals. In a separate bowl mix together milk, honey, and oil, and beat in egg. Add liquid ingredients to dry and stir. Batter should be fairly wet and lumpy. Pour into buttered bread tin or muffin tin. Bake at 400 degrees. A dozen muffins will take 20–25 minutes. Bread will take at least 25–30 minutes; at 25 minutes, check doneness with a toothpick. If it's still too moist, lower oven temperature and continue to bake, checking every 5 minutes to avoid overbaking.

THE HEADLESS SHRIMP OF DEWATTO POINT

DAVE WAITED UNTIL the canoe, a beastly scuffed-up war-
horse with a broken rib, was already offloaded from the top
of his truck to tell me that Dewatto Point, our chosen launch
among many possibilities, was known to Salish Indians as "the
place where evil spirits inhabit men's bodies." He'd borrowed
the canoe from a guy ten blocks down the street from his house.
In typical fashion he'd screeched to a halt outside the residence
where the forlorn craft was seemingly at its final resting place,
mostly obscured by weeds in a corner of the front yard. "Can
I borrow your canoe?" he'd shouted to a complete stranger in
his trademark manner of direct engagement. "Good thing you
asked today," the guy said. "I'm just the handyman. I don't live
here, but my boat does." Seventeen feet long, with a few streaks
of blue paint hanging on where it hadn't been scratched off on
rocks and sand. The day's rent for the vessel would be a dozen
shrimp. A bargain, we both agreed.

I've done stupider things than go shrimping in fifty-degree
water with a canoe, but mostly in my youth. "We're supposed
to know better by now," I said to Dave as we piled the traps and
buoys and buckets in before shoving off.

"Yeah," he grinned.

I'm one of those people who say they like to live by the
water, even though I don't own a boat and rarely have access to

one. Water is a comforting presence. It bathes the light and magnifies my emotions. I like to drive over the Ship Canal Bridge in Seattle and look west across the shimmery surface of Lake Union below, with its houseboats and floatplanes, and east to the slate blue of Lake Washington at the base of the Cascade foothills. The city's silver spires seem to grow out of the water like magnificent stalagmites. I like to watch low rain clouds scud across the horizon, marrying their load with the swells of Puget Sound. The water where I live is like a mirror reflection of the sky, a study in the infinite varieties of gray.

And yet, unlike Dave, I am not entirely at ease on or in the water. A feeling nags at me at such times, telling me I'm somewhere I don't belong—I'm trespassing.

Before launching I opened six cans of cat food (Friskies) and two cans of smoked shad (Tony's) and started packing the bait baskets. Anything we could do to lessen our bodily movements once aboard was a good thing.

"On the menu today we have salmon dinner, along with ocean whitefish in sauce and the captain's choice."

Dave looked at me with uncertainty. "No Puss 'n Boots?"

"Shrimp aren't brand conscious. Or they shouldn't be, anyway."

"The old salts swear by it."

"Well, the new salts have come to town." A pinkish slime of gooey fish products bled through the mesh of the bait baskets. I stuffed the two cylinders with one more can apiece for good measure. Each of these got hung inside a trap, a rectangular aluminum frame painted black, about three feet by three feet by a foot, with four narrowing entrances for the shrimp to pass through en route to the buffet. Rocks in each trap would keep them weighted down so they wouldn't "walk" on the bottom. Two spools of yellow nylon rope, 400 feet on each spool, were wound and ready to go. Two red and yellow buoys had our names and addresses written on them in indelible ink, according to law. After loading a wind sock, more bait, and an extra paddle, we were ready to launch. It was a few minutes before 9:00 AM. The fourth and last day of Hood Canal's spot shrimp season was about to open.

Shrimp, like so many good things, are bad for you. They're not unhealthy in a strict sense, like an intoxicant or a dose of mercury, but eating them indiscriminately can make you a bad person, or at least a lazy, uninformed consumer. The bottom line is this: if you eat imported wild shrimp—and the vast majority of shrimp eaten in the United States is both imported and wild—you're indirectly killing endangered sea turtles and a lot of other marine life forms. Farmed shrimp are no better, since the farms are hacked out of mangroves and other sensitive coastal habitats, their noxious wastes polluting surrounding soils and waterways.

What's a shrimp eater to do? I've loved shrimp for as long as I can remember, certainly stretching back further than 2001, the year shrimp surpassed canned tuna as the world's favorite seafood. It's hard to believe that the coveted crustaceans of my youth are now served on dinner plates and in Styrofoam fast-food containers across the globe. Shrimp used to be considered a luxury item nearly on par with lobster, but they're more affordable now, in large part because people have learned how to exploit their prolific abundance, and with that affordability comes a cost. According to Seafood Watch, while the shrimp themselves are not in any particular grave danger, unlike the targets of many other fisheries, buying shrimp in the market is still a dicey proposition for the environmentally conscious consumer. Shrimp are known by countless names, and their origin is often unclear. Keeping track of the "good" and "bad" varieties can be a chore even for the knowledgeable shrimp enthusiast. Most shrimp are imported from developing countries where regulations are scant and oversight even scanter, with bottom trawling the technology of choice. Trawling for shrimp kills nearly two million tons of additional marine life annually, accounting for more than 25 percent of the world's wasted catch. The bland industry term for this is "bycatch." The trawl nets are dragged across the seafloor, snaring everything in their path that isn't too small to slip through, including endangered sea turtles, sharks, fish, and invertebrates, which are tossed back overboard to die or be eaten. Some watchdogs put the figure at three to fifteen pounds of unwanted marine life killed for every pound of shrimp caught, making the shrimp fishery the worst bycatch offender in all commercial fishing.

Bottom trawling also disturbs the undersea habitat. In *The End of the Line*, British journalist Charles Clover asks readers to imagine "what people would say if a band of hunters strung a mile of net between two immense all-terrain vehicles and dragged it at speed across the plains of Africa." The result, in this apt analogy, is a "strangely bedraggled landscape resembling a harrowed field. There are no markets for about a third of the animals they have caught because they don't taste good or because they are simply too small or too squashed. This pile of corpses is dumped on the plain to be consumed by scavengers." Welcome to the shrimp trawling industry, the only difference being that the destruction happens underwater, out of sight, so consumers can conveniently use their seemingly limitless capacity for unimagination to ignore it.

Shrimp farming has its own costs. Mangroves and other coastal areas are being converted into farms, destroying the habitat in the process. The wastes accumulated on the farms damage surrounding waters, making some areas so polluted that they become dead zones. The shrimp themselves are often illegally shot up with antibiotics. Taras Grescoe suggests in his book *Bottomfeeder* that the widespread occurrence of seafood allergies may have more to do with reactions to foreign chemicals found in farmed shrimp than any naturally occurring compound in the shrimp themselves.

One way to eat shrimp responsibly is to catch your own. Wild-caught spot shrimp from United States waters earn a "good" ranking from Seafood Watch. The fishery is intensely

managed: in Washington State, spot shrimp were opened to recreational catch on Hood Canal for a total of four days last year.
Each spring, seafood lovers across the state wait to hear about
the fishery from the state's Department of Fish and Wildlife.
Some years it hardly opens at all; in a good year there might be
several scattered days. The personal limit is eighty shrimp per
day—enough to fill about half of a five-gallon bucket.

Up to ten inches in length, spot shrimp (*Pandalus platyc-
eros*) are the largest shrimp in Puget Sound. They're named for
the two pairs of white spots on their tail end. Otherwise they're
pinkish-orange or red, with a few white tiger stripes along the
carapace. Like other members of the crustacean order Decapoda,
including lobsters and crabs, they have five pairs of walking legs
along with three pairs of additional appendages used for eating
called maxillipeds. Shrimp are distinguished from other families
within Decapoda by five additional pairs of abdominal swimming legs called swimmerets. Spot shrimp, along with other
species in their family, have the distinction of being sex-change
artists. The shrimp hatch in early spring from eggs carried on
the female's legs. After a few months of a planktonic existence,
the larvae begin to resemble adults and, if conditions are stable
within the larger population, will mature into males. As adult
males they'll reproduce for a year or two before developing
female characteristics and extruding eggs. Once female, they'll
reproduce for another year or two and then die at the age of four
or five. Sometimes, in stressed or falling populations, some of the
shrimp will skip the male stage entirely and go straight to female
reproduction. This confusing life cycle would seem to be a good
way to ensure the survival of the species even in difficult times.
Spot shrimp feed on decaying matter and small sea creatures and
in turn are fed upon by larger bottom-feeders, including halibut,
lingcod, flounder, dogfish, and skates. In Hood Canal this means
they're a ways down there.

Hood Canal is not a canal at all. It's more like a fjord that's been airlifted out of Scandinavia and plunked down in Puget Sound. From its opening at Foulweather Bluff on the northern tip of the Kitsap Peninsula it extends southwest to the hamlet of Union, where it makes a sharp turn to the northeast like a fishhook—the Great Bend—and ends at the town of Belfair. The Olympic Mountains, which weren't officially traversed until the Press Expedition in 1890, the same year the U.S. Census declared the American frontier closed, rise up abruptly from the western shore like imposing, disgruntled guardians, giving the canal a dramatic backdrop of dark, sloping forests and snowy peaks. The canal is about sixty-five miles long, with an average width of a mile and a half and an average depth of 500 feet. The Vashon Glacier carved out Hood Canal before its retreat 15,000 years ago at the end of the Pleistocene Epoch. More recently, in 1792 during the first exploration of Puget Sound by a white man, Captain George Vancouver named the fingerlike body of water for one of his buddies, Lord Samuel Hood. Its cold, clear waters are home to a dazzling array of underwater life, although leaky septic systems and lax development codes have taken a toll on the once-pristine waters.

Though it's famous for its glassy, picture-perfect surface on calm days, powerful currents still run through Hood Canal, and in windy weather the conditions can be downright treacherous. Years ago, when my half-fish friend David Francis first told me he wanted to take a stab at the annual Hood Canal spot shrimp fishery, my initial question was this: How do you *dive* for shrimp? Dave brushed off this absurd notion with his usual impatience. "A boat," he said. "We get a boat." Was I hearing him correctly? This didn't seem like my friend at all. Never before had I witnessed him surrender to the impasse of water in something so conventional as a vessel. Water was to be parted and plumbed, not ridden on top of. Hundreds of recreational boaters descend on this short season each year, with twin-engine powerboats, electric winches, and all the attendant hoopla. It was hard to imagine Dave joining such a motorized scene. You can go down to the local fish market and buy spot shrimp for a lot less than many of these folks will eventually spend to have the experience of playing commercial fisherman for a day. That's when he mentioned the canoe. Ah, the catch. I knew there was no way he would be approaching a tradition as time-honored as recreational shrimping from any direction other than deep left field.

That first attempt is now etched in memory, if not seared by the elements. The canoe, a Mad River white-water variety, turned out to be surprisingly sea-worthy. We took it on a test drive around Dabob Bay, paddling up and down the shoreline, and then, satisfied with its conduct, ventured out deeper before returning to collect our pots. Meanwhile, there was a long line of trucks and trailers waiting to use the boat launch. This amused Dave to no end; he had a big grin on his face as we beached the canoe with a gravelly thud. A heavyset man in a dirty tank top with a salmon head in each hand gave us his opinion as he watched us maneuver the canoe back onto dry ground. "You're smiling now, but you boys are crazy. Plum crazy."

"Did you see us out there?" Dave challenged. "We turned her on a dime. This is the beginning of a movement. Next year, everyone will be in canoes."

"Hell, I'll give you some of mine. I don't even eat shrimp. The wife does. You'll get yourself killed." He laughed. He had to give Dave credit. *Crazy as a loon.* Dave smiled broadly, thinking it a compliment.

On that day Dave's wife Lesley was with us. She looked concerned. Lesley is the sensible one in the marriage. She holds down a steady job at a well-known coffee company and tries to keep Dave out of trouble. When Dave and Lesley first moved to Seattle from Maryland, Dave came out solo to scout for an apartment. He piled all their belongings into a barely running conversion van that he had picked up for next to nothing for the move west. In order to start the van, he had to light a match to the ignition and touch a couple of bare wires together. Lesley was so worried about her fiancé getting stranded that she came up with a plan. Dave was to keep the motor running at all times, even at fuel stations. They jerry-rigged a long piece of surgical tubing so that one end passed through a rust hole beneath the driver side door; the other end was fitted to a plastic half-gallon Coke bottle with the bottom cut off. Now Dave didn't have to worry about the engine conking out during a pee stop. "I evacuated my bladder on the fly," he told me triumphantly.

With ten minutes to go, we shoved off the beach for our maiden shrimping voyage and started paddling. We could hear Lesley calling Dave's name from the distance. "Don't do anything stupid out there," she hollered. Most of the other boaters were too busy fidgeting with their winches and whatnot to see us slip between them like attacking Indians. Five minutes before the start, we were several hundred yards offshore and scanning for a spot to drop our first pot. Without a depth finder, we had no idea how deep the water was. Wind speed and currents played into the computations as well, in ways that we could merely guess at.

"This is the place," Dave announced suddenly. "We'll drop the first pot here." It seemed like a good enough spot to me. We were within shouting distance of a couple of other boats should anything unfortunate happen. He readied the pots, working with the grave demeanor of a buccaneer preparing for battle, a huge sailor's knife locked between his teeth, mumbling orders out of the corner of his mouth. Though it was still spring, with mostly cold, wet weather in the Northwest, he already had a deep tan.

Nine o'clock. The sounds of splashes echoed across the water as hundreds of boats started dropping their pots. Dave flung ours away from the canoe and we watched it rock back and forth on the surface, then quickly flood with water and sink down out of sight. The water looked cool and inviting as it enveloped and took away the pot. I let the abrasive nylon rope slip through my gloved hands and tried to estimate the depth. When the rope stopped, we set the buoy. During the entire procedure, we drifted maybe a hundred yards with the current. Next, we paddled to another spot not too far away and repeated the process. Now all we had to do was wait.

It was a nice day for May, a little blustery, with wind out of the north. Many of the boaters around us were popping their first beers of the day and catching some rays. Women wore bikini tops. Dave and I decided to take our canoe on a more involved test drive. With help from a steady breeze, we rode the incoming tide to the south. The canoe handled nicely in the chop, catching waves like a kayak, its nose up on a plane. In the aft, Dave used his paddle like a rudder to make minor adjustments. We rode the rip and before long had rounded Quatsap Point, where the Duckabush River empties into the canal. It was time to go back.

We had to be careful executing our turn. The water was getting testier, with whitecaps starting to form farther out. A large swell hitting us broadside could swamp the canoe, or worse. I studied the patterns of waves and signaled Dave when it was time. Together we dug in with our paddles and made a quick pivot. Now, pointing north for the first time, we realized how much the wind had kicked up. I turned my ballcap backwards so it wouldn't blow away. Dave was chuckling in the back and churning his paddle. The muscles in his neck and shoulders stood out like thick cords. This was the sort of thing he lived for: nature throwing down the glove. I marked a rocky outcropping on the shore to my left. It neither advanced nor retreated; we were pulling our hardest and standing still.

With some experimenting we realized that synchronizing our strokes gained us a little extra momentum. The rock pile started to slip by ever so slowly, and then we were rounding the point again. What had taken a few minutes in one direction took nearly an hour in the other. We arrived back at Dabob Bay wet and exhausted, hardly ready for the physical ritual of pulling the first pot.

Without the element of danger, it almost wasn't worth it for Dave. Recently he had taken vacation right in the middle of his semester. He got a substitute teacher and pretended to be sick. He flew down to the Baja and drove around solo, camping on deserted beaches and spearing exotic fish for dinner. I told him he was asking to be caught—to be fired. But he just looked at me as if I were from a foreign country, speaking a funny language. "You don't understand," he said. "I had to go."

By the end of the day, with a few pulls on each pot, we had approached—but fallen short of—our limit. I could tell Dave was irked. Other shrimpers gathered on the beach to see our catch and offer encouraging words. Most of them had limited out, so they could be generous with the nutty canoers. "You fellas did well, considering," one said judiciously, gesturing with his tallboy. Already a scene was forming in the parking lot. Sunburned boaters relaxed in beach chairs outside their RVs. Camp stoves fired up. Pots on the boil. I could smell the shrimp turning orange.

We got our own pot going too. Lesley spiced the water and we cooked up a batch right on the beach. Dave was thinking of putting on his wetsuit to go for a dive at Seal Rock. There were oysters to shuck, too. It was late afternoon and the light was spectacular, a million shades of gray shot through with golden rays. At times like this, I wanted to sink down into the warm sand and never come up.

That was many years ago. Since then we've taken several boat rides, each time in a different canoe that Dave has managed to scavenge for the occasion, but never in one sporting an obvious structural flaw. Don't worry, he assured me now. Despite missing a rib, our rental canoe was built to withstand serious altercations. "Look at all those dings and scratches on the hull," he pointed out. "Badges of honor, each and every one. She's seen far worse than us. As long as we keep paddling, we'll be fine." He took a pull off a bottle of Maker's Mark and tossed in his life jacket. Whatever bad vibes might be hanging around Dewatto Point, waiting for an opportunity to inhabit our souls, he wasn't about to let a questionable canoe get in the way.

An hour later, we made our first pull of the day. Dave took the honor. He stood in the stern while I paddled to keep us in position. Standing in a canoe to pull up a shrimp pot is less precarious than one might think. The rope acts as a stabilizer, almost like leaning against a wall. Hundreds of feet down is the trap, weighted with stones and behaving more like an anchor. Each hand-over-hand retrieve collects another yard of rope in the canoe. You start with high hopes, with visions of dancing shrimp and all the meals you'll make with them: bouillabaisse, ceviche, shrimp risotto, fried shrimp. The list goes on. And so does the rope. Coils of it land around your ankles in the increasingly wet bottom of the canoe. Just when you think it will go on forever, the trap hoves into view.

"Surfacing!" Dave called out. I leaned over to see. The trap bubbled to the surface and spilled its water like an overflowing bathtub. Inside the trap, two dozen or more giant spot shrimp clicked around awkwardly. Dave threw open the cage and started grabbing shrimp by the fistful and dropping them in the bucket. It was a good first pull. The second pot, however, was a goose egg, and the third and fourth were just so-so. Already it was past noon and we weren't even close to filling our limits. We had two more pulls before the one o'clock closure.

Just then a small powerboat carrying two elderly couples motored over to us. They had limited and wanted to know if we wanted the contents of their last pot. "You can do the honors," said a gray-haired man in orange rubber hip waders, extending his hand for me to come aboard. Unlike most of the other shrimpers, they didn't have an electric winch—but they had the rope on a pulley, which made for a much easier pull. As I brought up their pot, the women were busy decapitating live shrimp and tossing the heads overboard. "Otherwise they spoil," one explained.

"That's not the real reason," the other said. "If you don't separate the head from the body, the ghost of the shrimp will come after you. The Indians believed that."

"I like to eat the head," I said cheerfully.

They looked at me with scrunched-up faces. "You want our heads?"

It was a tempting offer—I could make a lot of stock from all those shrimp heads—but the legalities were questionable. In any event, their last pot had a good thirty-five or forty shrimp in it, which we poured into our bucket before I climbed back into the canoe.

"How you doing anyway?" the man at the helm asked.

"Not too bad," Dave jumped in. "Pulled about two dozen in our first pot."

"Well, you boys have fun out here. Wind might come up soon." They motored off carefully, making sure not to leave much wake, looking back at us as they went.

In the end we failed to fill our limit once again, but only by five shrimp apiece, including the gifts. It was time to paddle in. After a half-day of pulling pots by hand, the takeout looked less than welcoming. We had used these same rickety wooden steps to carry the canoe down to the water earlier that morning, but now they looked steep and slippery, an accident waiting to happen. A hundred yards to the right was a low-bank beach that would make for an easy exit.

"To starboard," I called out. Dave noticed the old weathered signpost planted in the sand. The sign was blank.

"It's posted."

"Can you read it? I don't see any words."

He shrugged. "Okay, then, but actual words have no importance in this equation."

We beached the canoe and started unpacking the gear. Pretty soon a small boat carrying four middle-aged men dressed like loggers—old salts, to be sure—cut across the channel and pulled up in front of us. They would have looked comical—like a miniature car full of clowns—if they hadn't had such severe expressions pulling at their faces. "Do you know the owners?" one called out.

We looked at them. They were in a boat; we were on land. The canoe was on the truck, tied down. All we had to do was throw the rest of our stuff in the back.

"Course you don't!" he answered his own question after getting no reply. "We're the owners. We own this whole stretch of beach, me and my brothers here." He gestured with his hand, bringing all of Dewatto Point into his grasp with a sweep of his arm.

Another brother started yelling and raising his fists. He could hardly get the accusations out fast enough. "We saw you out there. You launched at the public launch this morning. Not good enough now? Need to trespass, do you?"

There wasn't much we could say. We were caught red-handed. It was only a matter of escalation now. I stepped forward. "You're right. We were tired, so we paddled over here where the bank was lower. It's our mistake." The strategic use of honesty caught the men off guard.

"We got ripped off this winter," one of them said. "Took all our oysters. Gone."

"We wouldn't do that. Just trying to get the boat out of the water."

"We oughta come up there and take your stuff."

The one with his hand on the tiller hushed his brothers. "He's just kidding you." The other men started to laugh, and now they were all laughing uproariously. "Putting the fear into you is all."

Dave and I started to join the laughter uneasily.

"Yeah, I'm just foolin'."

"He's the asshole in the family."

"Yeah, don't mind me. I'm an asshole."

"Don't do it again is all."

Just then an old woman in a golf cart drove up.

"Uh-oh, now you're really in trouble. You think we're bad—wait till you meet Grandma." They puttered off, laughing and waving. Grandma slowed to look at us.

"We're leaving," I said. She nodded and drove on.

Back at home, sore and tired, all I could muster in the kitchen was a quick tempura fry job—with the heads on, no less. Martha came over, expecting a genteel shrimp cocktail. I explained that the Chinese considered the head a delicacy. "Salt and pepper shrimp, like at the Hing Loon," I said. But after what was indeed a delicious meal, head and all, the Dewatto Point spot shrimp visited Martha that night in her dreams. She woke up early the next morning in a sweat, as if trying to claw her way out of a nightmare, restless and fatigued. "They've gone and inhabited my soul," she said with resignation. "The shrimp are swimming around inside me, and there's nothing I can do."

I propped myself up on my elbows. "I know just the thing. A head-on shrimp bouillabaisse. You'll love it."

SHELLFISH STEW

This dish can put even an enterprising seaside forager to the test. Squid, clams, and mussels are all available in Puget Sound and elsewhere during the fall and winter months, and spot shrimp caught in spring can be freed from the deep freeze. Sea scallops are a bit more difficult, although a free-diving friend of mine occasionally finds rock scallops, which he pries off the bottom in heroic feats of breath-holding. Marcella Hazan calls this recipe All-Shellfish and Mollusks Soup in her Essentials of Classic Italian Cooking. *True, if something of a mouthful. I call it simply Shellfish Stew. My version differs from Marcella's with its use of whole shrimp in the shell, which add flavor and look nice swimming around on top, and more tomatoes. Shellfish Stew is similar to other classic seafood soups with its fresh shellfish and tomatoes, but it differs from a traditional cioppino in its lack of finned fish. Like a bouillabaisse, which is a Provençal version of cioppino, Shellfish Stew is served over a thick slice of toasted crusty bread.*

And don't forget the leftovers: you have instant shellfish pasta.

½ cup olive oil
½ cup chopped yellow onion
1 tablespoon minced garlic
3 tablespoons chopped fresh parsley
   plus additional for garnish
1 cup dry white wine
1 large can (28 ounces) plum tomatoes, chopped, with juice
2 pounds whole squid
2 dozen or more live littleneck clams
1 dozen live mussels
1 pound fresh whole shrimp in shell,
   with tails sliced lengthwise for easy removal
1 pound fresh scallops
Salt and freshly ground black pepper to taste
Pinch red pepper flakes (optional)
Good crusty bread, sliced thick and toasted

Sauté onions in oil on medium heat until translucent. Add garlic. When garlic is golden, add parsley. Stir, then pour in wine and let bubble for half a minute before adding tomatoes with juice. Simmer for 10 minutes, stirring occasionally.

Meanwhile, clean squid and slice into rings (see instructions on pages 37-38); leave tentacles attached and whole if small. Scrub clams and mussels.

Add squid and cook at a gentle simmer for 45 minutes. Add water if necessary.

Season stew, then add shrimp. Simmer 5 minutes before adding clams and mussels and turning up heat to high. Stir. As clams and mussels begin to open, add scallops. Cook until all clams and mussels are open. Ladle into large soup bowls, over toasted bread, and garnish with chopped parsley. SERVES 6–8

UP FROM THE ASHES, FIRE FRUIT

BECAUSE MY FRIEND Cora likes a good meal, preferably cooked with fresh local ingredients, he didn't need much convincing when I suggested we drive to the far side of the mountains and stomp around in a graveyard. Cora is a gourmet cook, and I figured at the least our trip would lead to a delicious meal. After consulting maps and working the phones, we decided to camp north of Winthrop, Washington, not far from the Canadian border, where the previous summer a 175,000-acre wildfire had ripped through surrounding forest. The plan was to hike across miles of charred-over pine and fir at an elevation of around 4,000 feet—and find dinner.

Why would we want to walk around in mud and ash in the midst of millions of dead, twisted trees to whet our appetites? Well, because we suffered from an acute case of morel madness.

Morels are among the most highly esteemed of the wild mushrooms, more coveted than chanterelles or even that pricey Japanese favorite, the matsutake. This is reflected in their market price. Fresh morels command top dollar, and even last season's well-preserved specimen—like a mint 1965 Mustang—goes for a healthy sum. Many gourmands would argue, in fact, that dried morels, aged to concentrate their earthy aroma and reconstituted in wine, cream, or stock, are more sublime than the freshest of just-picked.

This gustatory appeal is not immediately clear on first glance.

To look at a morel is to be confronted by a suspiciously obvious phallic symbol, a gag played by Mother Nature. Indeed, the great father of modern taxonomy Linnaeus described the morel as a "phallus with an egg-shaped head" and gave it the scientific name *Phallus esculentus*—basically, tasty phallus. Though highly variable in shape, size, and color, the average morel stands a few inches tall with a conical head perched on a smooth, cream-colored stalk. The head is deeply ridged and pitted, giving it a bizarre honeycombed look that is almost sentient, as if the morel has a mind of its own. Cookbook author and all-around culinary whiz James Beard has called it the look of dried-up brains. While the scent has been described as a complex mix of earth and raw milk, the taste is harder to articulate: smoky, nutty, woodsy… fecund. Legendary gourmand and newsman R. W. Apple described them as "musky, loamy, faintly sweet, hinting of caraway and bell peppers." Bell pepper seems a reach, but depending on the locale where it was foraged, the morel can be many things to many people. Always, when cooked right, it exhibits that *al dente* texture that is the hallmark of so many beloved foods, from shrimp to asparagus.

Today morels are classified in the *Morchella* genus, a genus as poorly understood by scientists as it is admired by chefs. No one knows how many individual species of morel there are, and there is some disagreement about even the known species. Most of the Latin names derive from the Old World and may or may not apply to North American morels (the verdict from DNA testing is still mostly out). Both mycologists (fungi scientists) and mycophagists (fungi eaters) refer instead to general color distinctions. There are blacks, blonds, yellows, whites, greens, grays, pinks, and reds, and within these groups there are both naturals and burn morels. The naturals are the morels prized by midwesterners, who convene annually in the month of May to pay homage at morel festivals all over Michigan, Illinois, Indiana, and elsewhere. Their morels are relatively consistent—if you know where to find them—behaving more, well, naturally. Which is to say that naturals pop up in the places you'd expect them to each spring, in more or less the same numbers, cyclically and predictably, if still not easy to find.

Then there are the ones you find in burns. These are the jack-in-the-boxes of chaos theory, the mushrooms of disturbance and destruction—as well as rebirth. Burn morels most famously thrive in the aftermath of forest fires and logging operations, when they sometimes fruit in unimaginable numbers. This was the variety we would be seeking out.

Each spring across the North American West, morel hunters scrutinize maps of the previous year's wildfires. If conditions look right, they flock to these unearthly barbecue pits in droves, on the promise of prolific crops of burn morels. Researchers don't know for sure, but they believe such massive fruitings are a result of the fungus, most of which lives underground in the form of nutrient-sucking tendrils called mycelia, making a last-ditch effort to reproduce after the death of its host tree. The mushroom is the fruiting body of the fungus and is responsible for spreading the reproductive spores of future generations. The morel's strategy, it would seem, is to blanket the scorched earth with its spores and hope that a few get borne away to friendlier places on the wind or carried on the backs of birds and insects. Or spilled from the basket of a hungry mushroom hunter.

On a hot July day, lightning strikes ignited the tinder-dry Okanogan National Forest six miles northeast of Winthrop, on the edge of the Pasayten Wilderness. With conditions exacerbated by beetle-killed lodgepole pines, a conflagration quickly erupted near Tripod Peak. The Tripod Complex, as the fire came to be known, roared through at least a dozen containment lines, threatening to consume the mountain hamlets of Conconully and Loomis, and was battled by more than 2,000 fire-fighting personnel from as far away as Mexico and New Zealand before heavy winter snows finally quelled its flames.

The fire was still smoldering when mushroom pickers

around the Northwest began anticipating its regenerative pow-
ers. I went online to see what I could learn. The Forest Service,
forever strapped for cash to repair storm-damaged trails and
overused campgrounds, had somehow managed to put together
a special online brochure for would-be mushroom pickers—and
in no fewer than four languages, including Spanish, Laotian, and
Khmer. The brochure included a map of the fire zone and directions to two commercial mushroom "camps" in the Okanogan
National Forest. These camps, I had heard, would become like
small cities at the peak of the season, with hundreds of inhabit-
ants and even a support crew of scrappy entrepreneurs serving
up $5 plates of pad Thai and the like from open-air soup kitch-
ens. Like any microcosm of society, the camps would not be
without their antisocial elements. Reports from similar commercial camps in the past had detailed the intense competition
and even violence between different ethnic groups. Some pickers
carried weapons to protect themselves and enforce what they
considered to be the laws of the woods. They patrolled territories
and boundaries, never mind that this was all happening on public land. I had heard stories of turf wars breaking out, with wild
running gun battles raging through the forest.

On another site for buyers and pickers, I left a message for
the mycognoscenti, asking how a recreational hunter like me
might approach the burn. I wanted to find mushrooms, but I
didn't want to tangle with a possessive picker or walk into the
middle of a firefight. One helpful fellow, who went by the handle
"Chickenofthewoods," replied that I should scout the roads for
likely "shroommobiles"—old vans and pickups—and then park
a respectful distance away before entering the burn. Another,
stung by my recreational status—which removed me from the
economic roller-coaster of the commercial picker and therefore
made me less than serious—bristled at the idea of identifying
mushroom pickers on the roadside. Commercial pickers are the
ones "standing by a 1978 Toyota pickup eating raw hotdogs
while taking a break from six hours of work," he wrote. "The

recreational pickers are standing by a Land Rover eating Brie and looking worried about getting their new boots dirty!"

As a new member of the Puget Sound Mycological Society, I couldn't have disagreed more. The urban mushroom hunters I had met so far were an eccentric lot—heavy on Eastern European and Mediterranean immigrants—who enjoyed nothing more than spending days on their knees in the dirt looking for edible fungi. They were hardly the fleece-clad outdoor enthusiasts of the New West, and the fact that they didn't traffic in mushrooms had nothing to do with their savvy in the woods or what kind of junkers they drove.

My friend Cora, though not a member, would fit right in. He has roots in the northern Italian region of Piedmont, which he honors above all with his choices of food and drink. Once, while house-sitting his cat, I came across a bottle of grappa tucked away in a closet and had a few snorts. Later I learned that the homemade liquor was the last extant bottle from his dearly departed grandfather's stash. Cora shrugged and said I better have appreciated it.

Cora's first name is Chris, though he's been called by his last name for as long as I've known him. Even his wife, Lori, calls him Cora sometimes, which is funny, since that's her name now, too. Maybe Cora should have taken hers instead, because everyone knows that Lori is the pitch between the timbers on the good ship Cora. Lori is a lawyer with the EPA and given to rational thinking; Chris is an epicure and potter and given to protracted argument and relentless devil's advocacy. His weakness for good drink and disputation takes him deep into black holes—and Lori is always ready to toss a lifeline. Once, at the end of a very late night, Lori famously said, "I circumnavigate the outer realms searching for my husband." And when she finds him, on whatever distant comet, she faithfully—and in good humor—reels him in. It's an enviable marriage.

I met the Coras at a bar one night to discuss our morel-hunting plans. They had recently returned from a trip to Italy and,

perhaps in a fit of jealousy, I made the mistake of referring to the
Boot as a third-world country, prompting a long, wistful polemic
from Cora about the upsides of graft and corruption and ending
with the loud pronouncement that "good things get done in Italy,
one way or another."

"That's precisely it," I countered. "Things *don't* get done in
Italy anymore, good or otherwise."

"Yes," he said, "but in not doing things, Italy maintains its
character."

There was no way to win these arguments with Cora.

What we *could* agree on was to put aside the weekend after
Memorial Day for our trip. Unlike in the Midwest, where the
morel fruiting keeps a tight schedule between late April and
May, these mushrooms would be at a higher elevation in the
mountains; we wanted to arrive at the burn site not long after
snowmelt when the flush was fresh, and ideally before the bulk
of the commercial harvesters descended on it.

Leaving the bar after all this morel talk, I wanted nothing
more than to go home and fry up a steak and morel dinner, but
the cupboard was bare.

The culinary history of morels is sketchy at best. We know that
ancient Romans collected morels. We also know that the royal
kitchens of Europe had a fondness for them, although not much
is known about how the mushrooms were prepared in the
Middle Ages or the Early Modern Period. Both the nobility and
the peasantry ate morels. According to *The Oxford Companion
to Food*, eighteenth-century German peasant women became
destructive firebugs in their zeal to promote the heath fires that
would encourage morel fruitings. Around this same time, English
agriculturist Richard Bradley wrote in *The Country Gentleman
and Farmer's Monthly Director* (1727) that "morilles" were "so
single a rarity" that he could not avoid "acquainting the Farmer
of their excellence, that he may not pass them by as things to
be disregarded, for they make an excellent Dish either broil'd or

stew'd." When sautéed morels and shallots were first combined with cream to make the signature dish is even less clear. Georges Auguste Escoffier, perhaps the original celebrity chef, includes several morel recipes in *Le Guide Culinaire* (1903), including Morilles à la Crème. Pellegrino Artusi, on the other hand, makes no mention of morels in his magnum opus, *Science in the Kitchen and the Art of Eating Well* (1891), which may have more to do with nationalist pride, porcini being the wild mushrooms of choice in Italy.

Early American cookbooks have little to say about wild mushrooms at all, although Fannie Merritt Farmer avers in her *Boston Cooking-School Cook Book* (1896) that they "may be easily gathered, and as they contain considerable nutriment, should often be found on the table." Nowadays, despite its omission from *The Joy of Cooking*, there are whole cookbooks devoted to the morel. The queen of California nouvelle cuisine, Alice Waters, cooks with morels at Chez Panisse. So does Daniel Boulud (of Le Cirque fame) in New York. Particularly in the Midwest, where there's a thriving morel culture, one can find any number of locally published books and pamphlets paying homage to the spongy mushroom of spring.

Perhaps it's only fitting that such knowledge be local. Mushroom tasting presents the ultimate case of trial and error, with the costs of error far outweighing any benefits, at least for the taster, and it is only recently, with the advent of more comprehensive field guides, that mushroom hunting has been raised above the level of folklore. Even with access to the best information, morels resist easy harvest; there's no substitute for the on-the-ground knowledge that comes from getting to know a place and its scraggly edges—which is why serfs could eat morels as readily as their lords hundreds of years ago, and why you can get a bowl of morel chowder in season at a Michigan diner that's every bit as fresh and wonderful as one at the most expensive French restaurant.

However they are prepared, one thing is certain: unlike your typical supermarket mushroom, which can be eaten raw, morels must be cooked to prevent poisoning. Seventy-seven diners found this out the hard way recently at a banquet in Vancouver, British Columbia, when a highfalutin yet ultimately ignorant chef served uncooked morels in a salad course, resulting in a mass case of gastroenteritis, or stomach flu. Such toxicity is banished with a little flame, making fresh wild morels delicious in almost any preparation involving heat, whether battered and fried, stuffed and broiled, or, of course, sautéed.

In *The Mushroom Feast* (1975), the first truly contemporary book devoted to mushroom cookery, Jane Grigson includes a recipe for Flan of Morels à la Crème that can only be called modernist. She explains that the recipe was adapted from the *Alice B. Toklas Cook Book* and was almost certainly made with morels because Gertrude Stein had presented the hotel cook with the bounty of a springtime walk taken northwest of Chartres. If a flan is more work than you bargained for, a simple morel cream sauce poured over meat or pasta is perhaps the most enduring way to enjoy these "tasty phalluses."

I had been thinking—perhaps obsessing is the right word—about morel cream sauces since late winter, when my stash ran out. Surely I could have ventured into some stuffy gourmet imported-food store and spent a small fortune on some dried morels of dubious origin, but such a transaction would have only piqued my desire. No, I needed to get out into the woods and find some for myself so I could indulge in one of my favorite artery stoppers: grilled veal chop smothered in morel-tarragon cream sauce. With a nod to the French and their infamous reputation for dodging the bullet of heart disease, I would draft numerous red wines into the campaign.

Moreover, I had promised my parents that when I saw them in June I would be packing a large quantity of the mushrooms. Normally Mom and Dad are careful about their diets. They've reached an age when prudence is the better part of culinary valor. Each new year now, beginning on January 1 and extending

through the month, they "put on the hair shirt" and swear off
alcohol. They eat a lot of greens year-round and keep fatty foods
to a minimum. They absolutely refuse such decadent fare as rich
creamy dishes. But the appeal of morel cream sauce over young
succulent cow cannot be denied. I wondered how I would get
all the morels on the plane. I was planning to travel light; the
idea of checking bags through to the circus tent that is Denver
International Airport was out of the question. I could already see
the look on the X-ray attendant's face as he studied my carry-on.
Yep, those are mushrooms. Is that a problem?

On a Friday before the Seattle rush hour, I rendezvoused with
the Coras to head east over the mountains. Because he is a Trek-
kie, Cora naturally drives a vehicle known as the Transporter, a
blue '87 VW camper-van with a lone bumper sticker on the rear
acquired at Malheur Wildlife Refuge, warning other drivers that
he "Brakes for Birds." This was his most recent in a long line of
VWs stretching back to the original air-cooled, bubble-shaped
microbus (equipped in those days with bumper stickers more
along the lines of "I Brake for Hallucinations"), and it was tricked
out with all the comforts he needed on the road, including a
hand-built cherrywood console designed to hold large cups of
coffee and a lot of CDs. Buddha was lying in the back on a dog-
gie mattress, his muzzle between his forepaws, looking worried
the way retrievers do. Lori produced a sheaf of maps.

The Tripod Complex was about four hours away. We drove
through North Cascades National Park on Route 20, which had
recently reopened after avalanche season. The squirrelly, largely
two-lane gawker summits two mountain passes—Rainy and
Washington—before dropping into the Methow Valley on the dry
east side of the Cascade Crest. It's one of the most beautiful and
awe-inspiring drives in the world, chockablock with glaciated
peaks and jagged vistas, but we weren't out for scenery. We had
to compete with the hordes of weekend warriors scrounging for
a campsite—and, worse, the numerous commercial mushroom

pickers who were already converging on the Tripod.

By the time we reached the Wild West tourist town of Winthrop, it was nearly dark. We turned north where the Chewuch River empties into the Methow, following the tributary up into Okanogan National Forest. The river was high and off-color. I had fly-fished for little pan-sized rainbow trout in this stretch before. Soon the spring run of chinook salmon would arrive like an invading army and start pushing the other fish around as if they owned the place. In the half-light of dusk, the ridges looked like fake, two-dimensional backdrops, Potemkin mountains hiding their unseen fungal guests. Unlike the steep, ice-carved west flank of the Cascades, the eastern side is gentler, more like the Rockies, with rolling slopes and open country suitable for off-trail travel. Ponderosa and lodgepole pine predominate on the drier hillsides, while the Douglas fir forests stick to the wetter creek bottoms and north-facing slopes. It's some of the wildest land left in Washington, home to the few wolves and grizzlies still hanging on in the state. Under the load of a backpack, I'd seen most of the drainages in the Pasayten Wilderness at least once—though without an eye for morels.

After a quick dinner of shish kebabs grilled over a campfire and a drink of whiskey, we got out the maps. It didn't take long to see that we all had different notions about where the morels would be flourishing. "I think we should go here," Cora said, pointing to a spot on the map apropos of nothing.

"Why there?"

"Because it looks good."

Lori jumped in. "I think we should decide in the morning, when we're not squinting around a gaslight." At that moment an enormous moth called a California silkworm careened into the lamp with a loud thwack and alighted on the map. Cora noted the moth's coordinates and said that would be our destination tomorrow. This was just like him. "Leave it to the cosmic forces," he said gravely. I was in no mood to argue. It was time to go to bed, visions of plump morels dancing in our heads.

The next morning a life-sized portrait of Jerry Garcia stepped wearily from the van and regarded me through kaleidoscopic granny glasses.

"We're not looking for *those* mushrooms, Cora."

"It's my lucky t-shirt. What time is it?" It was already getting late. In an hour the sun would be over the ridge and hot. We ate instant oatmeal and vacated our campsite. Armed with maps, compasses, a GPS unit, walkie-talkies, knives, brushes, and the low-tech wicker baskets that gave our little band a pastoral flair, we pointed the Transporter toward the blast zone, driving down-stream along the Chewuch and crossing a bridge where Boulder Creek's rushing torrent joined the river. A dirt road contoured high above the creek's gorge, offering glimpses down into a river bottom shaded by a lush green canopy of cottonwood, alder, and Douglas fir. RVs and pickups occupied every pullout and guer-rilla camping spot. Blue tarps and multicolored tents decorated the forest.

"Mushroom pickers behind every stump," Cora muttered.

Evidence of small spot fires came into view—patches of for-est with red needles and blackened ground cover. We turned a corner and the devastation opened up before us: entire hillsides reduced to ash. The sight was shocking. Where the fire had burned hottest, nothing remained but the javelin-shaped spars of a few remaining tree trunks, coal black and bereft of branches. Here the fire had whipped up windstorms that uprooted entire trees and touched off explosions in the crowns. The earth was pockmarked as if it had endured a prolonged shelling.

This was the red zone, as indicated by our Forest Service map of the fire. It smelled like the inside of a chimney. From the car, the red zone looked to be an impossible bet.

"This is it," Cora announced. He'd been morel hunting exactly once in his life.

"Are you sure?" Lori asked. I was less politic. I denounced his confidence immediately and suggested we ought to look for transition zones—marked yellow on the map—where the fire hadn't been so all-consuming. Cora agreed somewhat reluctantly, and we drove up the road looking for just the right place. When we finally put boots to the ground, the first thing we found was the bleached bones of some large animal caught in the fire, a deer, I figured, although Cora pronounced it a cow. He kicked a femur and it fell apart like spent charcoal briquettes. The two of us stepped over the skeleton and raced each other into the woods while Lori stayed behind near the van.

Morels, as any mushroom hunter knows, are a conundrum. The sad fact is that they're notoriously hard to find. It takes years of optical training to consistently see them, even right before your eyes. Like fungal chameleons, they possess an uncanny ability to mimic their surroundings. If fruiting in a healthy conifer forest, they look like drab little pinecones lounging in the duff; among the ash and charred remains of a burn, they take on the mordant hues of incineration. Even seasoned morel hunters regale each other with stories about the morel they saw at fifteen paces—and then searched for in vain on hands and knees for the next hour. Getting your "eyes on" is a requirement and an almost mystical warm-up routine, like doing a bunch of deep knee-bends or a few jumping jacks before an athletic contest. With your eyes on, you can see the morels hiding all around, like looking at trout in a riffle through polarized sunglasses.

More mysterious than the actual seeing is the locating. Rarely will morels fruit in the same place for more than a couple of seasons. Trying to deduce their preferred habitat and timing is a year-round parlor game for mushroom hunters. A complex algorithm of elevation, soil composition, temperature, humidity, slope aspect, and local vegetation must be mulled over. It's not uncommon to hear of a neophyte morel hunter spending an entire season or two without a single mushroom to show for it.

The seduction and elusiveness of morels impressed avant-garde composer John Cage. In a piece of music called "Indeterminacy," which matches ninety short-short stories written and read aloud by Cage with piano and prerecorded music, he tells about finding a morel in town, a "choice mushroom which is rare around Rockland County," and how "none of the people living on this street ever talk to me while I'm collecting mushrooms." The next year he returns to find that "a cinder-block house had been put up where the mushroom had been growing." One of the neighbors laughs at him. It's a telling detail. Mushroom hunters can be objects of derision. They wander the woods as if overcome by senility, hunched over, slowly taking one careful step after another so as not to miss anything, lost in their thoughts. Little do the bystanders understand. The mycophagists aren't doddering or daffy—they are like kids on a treasure hunt, patiently examining the clues around them, on the trail of edible ducats and doubloons.

For me, this needle-in-a-haystack characteristic is part of the enjoyment. Hunting for morels is like a great game of hide-and-seek in the woods, an Easter egg hunt of epic proportions. Still, I had entangled Cora in so many fishless fishing adventures in the past that I was nervous about proposing the morel hunt. What if, after all this driving around, we got skunked?

Ten minutes later, already frustrated and ready to give up on our first spot, we heard a shout from Lori, then another. Cora and I hurried back to find her still hovering over the animal bones. "It took me a while to focus," she said modestly. "And all along they were right here in front of me!"

She held up a perfect little morel in each hand. Slowing down now, I started seeing them all around, poking through the pine needles beneath a vertebra and concealed under burnt logs. We scoured an area the size of a hockey rink, lining our baskets and talking jovially. Cora could already taste the epicure's dream of simplicity: sliced morels sizzling in garlic and butter.

"Add some veal stock and cream to that," I said, licking my chops. "And a couple pinches of chopped fresh tarragon. Voilà, the best sauce for steak or veal you ever had."

Lori admired her basket. "I like mine on a cracker." And then, just like that, our first patch petered out all at once and it was time to move on. We each had only a single meal's worth. We needed more.

After lunch Lori and I gave in to Cora's speculations and tried one of the red zones. From the road these moonscapes looked uninhabitable, but once inside the charred ruins we found a multiplicity of life. Woodpeckers hammered on hollowed-out hulks still standing, and deer tracks crisscrossed the pumice-like earth. And the morels? They stuck up out of the ash like a crop of fire fruit. They grew sideways from stump holes and sprouted in the columns of shade behind burnt tree trunks. We sliced them off and moved through the burn like fungal undertakers.

Ski bums have an expression for those brief interludes when the conditions are transcendent: no friends on powder days. Once at the top, all chairlift camaraderie melts away as the powder hound picks his line and disappears into a plume of snow. And so it is with any pursuit that relies on the fickleness of the weather for its highest achievement, mushroom picking included. We spread out on the burned slopes, giving each other room, using the walkie-talkies not so much for safety as for keeping tabs. "Where are you? Finding anything over there? Any big ones?" In such a dynamic, a sense of competition develops. You notice each other's baskets and take inventory. You keep score. We had partaken of the wily morel, and though there was knowledge and pleasure to be gained from its study, there was also a fall from grace. This was no walk in the woods. We hurried furtively from spot to spot, each of us alone with our thoughts, hoping to uncover the mother lode around the next bend. No friends in fire zones.

I experienced within myself that antsy, restless feeling that is the result of only one thing: greed. I rushed around the blackened firescape searching for a bonanza that seemed so close at hand and yet remained tantalizingly out of reach. Ah, but this wasn't really greed, I argued with myself. After all, I had promised a load for my parents...and I needed some to share with the neighbors…and what about drying a batch for winter? Each morel made me yearn even more for the next one. Morel nirvana was just around the corner. I was racing the clock. A gallon of mushrooms—a basket *half empty!*—struck me as a piddling amount. The commercial pickers, after all, were pulling out poundage.

And we cursed them. The commercials were always a step or two ahead of us. Tire tracks tattooed each turnout like abstract Kilroys in the dirt. Footprints zigzagged through the ash. Some of the slopes showed evidence of multiple harvests, the telltale signs of cut stems barely visible in the singed duff. We wondered if the morels we had found were mistakes, stragglers left behind as the slope was otherwise vacuumed clean. Then we heard them: unfamiliar voices singsonging back and forth across the valley. They were all around us.

"We're not alone," I called to Cora on the walkie-talkie. "I think they've got us surrounded." Were we trespassing? How long before the shooting started?

Cora was too far along in his own morel mania to care. Evicted by some gun-toting mushroom hunter? Not likely. "If they're serious about staking a claim," he radioed back, "they'll squeeze off a few warning shots first." Besides, he was more concerned about his dog. "Buddha!" he started calling out, his voice echoing through the blackened forest. What did our antagonists think of that? We backtracked to the van just to be sure. Cora yelled again. "Buddha, come!" At that moment dog and picker appeared on the road at once. Buddha trotted over to us, unconcerned.

The picker was a small, lithe Asian man strapped into an enormous backpack that towered over him. The pack held several plastic crates stacked vertically. He looked at us quizzically and then crossed the road. Where was he going? We had already been on that side of the road earlier in the day, far up into a scorched drainage that had been picked clean. Was he going higher, maybe even up and over to the next drainage, where there wouldn't be a road and weekend pickers like ourselves? With that huge pack?

Cora took a swig of water and spat in the dust. "These guys don't carry guns." He strode over to confront the picker, to ask him how it was done, but the man was already disappearing into the burn. No time to talk. He made a gesture indicating that he didn't understand us and was gone. So much for gun battles.

Through it all, the sun beat down on us and the ruined forest offered no relief. Hands black with soot, faces smudged and sweaty, we investigated one likely draw after another. We tried to think as commercial pickers would, or as we imagined they would, sometimes driving for miles up a rough logging road before being turned away by a locked gate or washout. Tired, dirty, and hungry, we grew grumpy with each other and had difficulty making decisions about where to go. Each of us had developed our own theories about what sort of conditions promoted the best fruitings.

Despite Lori's early victories of patience, in the end it was Cora himself who became one with the mushroom. His morel mojo led him deeper and deeper into the burn. Whereas I harbored doubts and didn't want to waste too much time in areas that didn't seem promising, Cora took the approach of covering a spot in its entirety. With Buddha at his heels, he disappeared down a slope and out of radio contact, reemerging late that afternoon as the anointed, his basket overflowing with the largest, freshest morels of the trip. I looked at his haul with envy.

Then, at his moment of triumph, he announced that it was time to go. The clock had run out. We were dirty and needed to wash. More than that, we might have all felt just a little bit sheepish, each of us silently realizing that the mushrooms had gotten the best of us. Talking about the morels we would fry in garlic and butter back at camp couldn't quite get the bad taste out of our mouths, the taste of unchecked desire and competition and secrecy. Somehow, we needed to redeem ourselves.

We bumped back down the road, the late afternoon sun slanting in our eyes, and crossed paths with a single white Ford pickup. The driver slid to a stop in the gravel and rolled down his window. Cowboy hat, handlebar mustache. Dust and exhaust blew around.

"Doin' any good?"

"Not too bad," Cora said cryptically. It was an understood reality within the mushroom picking community that you never revealed your successes or secret spots. Even friends declined to share information with each other. No friends…

The driver looked perplexed. "Where you from?"

Seattle, we said, hearing maybe just a little bit of the city slicker in our voices.

A moon-faced woman in the passenger seat said they'd been poking around but had only a single mushroom to show for their efforts. Her husband looked slightly embarrassed at this admission. "We're locals," he went on, flashing a smile. "Just looking for enough to make a dinner is all."

At that moment we were all thinking the same thing. Cora switched off the engine and popped open a beer. "Well, in that case," he said, "let us tell you what we know."

VEAL CHOPS WITH MOREL CREAM SAUCE

Cream sauces need not be complicated. The simplicity of this recipe makes it perfect for a hearty, artery-busting dinner following a long day of foraging. (You earned it!) Use as much or as little of the stock and cream as desired. Substituting a good cut of steak such as rib-eye for the veal is permissible.

> 2 tablespoons butter
> 1 shallot, diced
> 20 or more medium to large morels, cleaned and chopped; leave small morels whole

¼ cup dry white wine
1 cup veal or beef stock (I use Glace de Viande Gold,
    usually available from quality markets)
½ cup or more heavy cream
1 tablespoon chopped fresh tarragon (or thyme or rosemary)
Salt and freshly ground black pepper to taste
1 teaspoon cornstarch (optional)
2 thick veal chops (or steaks)

Sauté shallot in butter for a minute or two on medium-high heat, then add morels and cook for 5 minutes. Deglaze with white wine. Reduce heat and slowly add stock and cream. Stir in seasonings. Simmer until desired thickness, a few minutes at a minimum. A teaspoon of cornstarch can hasten the thickening process if necessary.

Season veal chops, then grill or pan-fry. Suggested sides: rice pilaf and fresh spring asparagus. Serve with a good bottle of Cabernet or Zinfandel. SERVES 2

SUMMER

dungeness crab

CRAB FEED

WHEN FRIENDS FROM out of town come to visit, I like to give them the opportunity to feel awkward, get dirty, and maybe even impale themselves on a sharp object. I feed them crab. A fresh-caught mess of Dungeness crabs in the shell offers all these advantages, not to mention the reward of sweet, sought-after meat that is as much a feature of the West Coast as the blue crab is of the East—only better.

The setup is simple: newspaper on table, boiled crab on newspaper, beer in hand. There was a time when I melted sticks of butter and left a can of Old Bay out, but I'm over such garish additives now. Crab wants to be eaten *neat*.

Perhaps it's only fair to acknowledge the butter debate. I'll admit that I enjoy dunking lobster in hot melted butter as much as the next person, and I suppose it's not heresy to do the same with Dungeness. Certainly blue crab needs an extra boost, all the better with garlic and cream, but I usually refrain with our native Pacific crab. A fisherman I know insists on the cheater. "My dad taught me how to eat crab," Steve declared once, red in the face, when we were covering this ground yet again. "He'd have the ramekin of butter, and the big pieces he'd dip. The small pieces got tossed into the ramekin. Then at the end...." Steve paused to imagine the last bits of crab being stirred around in slightly congealed butter until they were all caught up on the tines of his fork. He sighed.

I'm not trying to ruin any childhood memories. Even I will eat Dungeness crab with butter on occasion. The point is, you don't have to. The meat is so succulent and pleasing to the palate in its suppleness that it can be eaten right out of the shell without even the slightest regret for a lack of condiment. Sucking the claws and legs of their juices is the very essence of eating Dungeness crab. When you eat crab with the right people, the room is filled with yips and low moans and slurping sounds and countless other audible expressions of ecstasy.

Invariably there's one guest who will insist on wearing a crab bib—just as his father or grandfather had years earlier—but I gave up long ago trying to prevent crab juice and fragments of shell from spraying me head to toe, never mind the newsprint that rubs off on hands and arms like smudgy prison tattoos. It's a dirty business, eating crab, and not for the squeamish. My only nod to my more fastidious guests is a roll of paper towels on the table.

You need a big pot for a mess of crabs—a bubbling cauldron, really. Such cookery brings out the witches and warlocks in us all, and I'll admit to taking some ghoulish pleasure in dragging credulous crab-eaters into the kitchen for the moment of truth: the tossing of live crabs into the boil. Though that high-pitched whine isn't really the screaming of the crabs but rather the sound of air whistling out of their shells, the effect is always the same. I feel bad about this moment, too. Really.

The cooked crabs are brought out on platters and dumped in the middle of the papered table. Armfuls of cold beer in the bottle are hustled out as well. Eating crab and drinking beer go hand in hand, and the more beer the less self-conscious the guests will be about cracking shells, ripping off claws, splattering each other, and combing through tall shell middens for elusive nuggets.

Breaking the cooked crabs down into edible chunks isn't as difficult as one might think. The carapace, fiery orange after boiling, is the first to go. It comes off easy with a little leveraging on the hindquarters. The guts will usually slide away with the shell, and what's left of them can be scraped off along with the lungs. After you snap the body in half, the two mirror sections are ready for eating. Each leg can now be separated as a segmented piece, with a good chunk of meat exposed at the joint where the leg was formerly attached to the body. Claws often require a cracker—or a swift blow from an empty beer bottle.

All this work is paid back handsomely. For the neophyte, the first bite is usually a revelation. How can a scuttling insect of the sea be so tender and delicious? Even seasoned crab eaters are stirred in primal, unexpected ways, making a crab feed a loose and unpredictable event.

Reputedly named after a small, defunct fishing village on the Strait of Juan de Fuca in Washington State, Dungeness crabs inhabit coastal waters from Alaska's Aleutian Islands to Monterey Bay, California. They can grow to ten inches across the carapace, though an eight-inch span is more common.

The crabs begin life by hatching out of eggs carried on the abdomen of the female in a mass known as a sponge, with a large female caring for up to two and a half million eggs. After hatching, the young are free-swimming, or planktonic. Over the next year they go through several larval, shrimplike stages before molting into their familiar crab form as juveniles.

Crabs are reproductively mature at two to three years. As adults they scavenge the bottom, feeding on clams, mussels, shrimp, small fish, and dead animals. They move into shallow water to mate in the spring, with the male clasping the female face to face in a sort of wrestler's clinch, waiting for her to molt so he can penetrate the soft abdomen and deposit his sperm. The female will then carry the sperm with her for up to several months, not fertilizing the eggs until she extrudes them from her abdomen, at which point she buries herself in the sand until the eggs hatch. Aside from humans, the crab's main predators include bottomfish such as halibut, dogfish, and sculpins, as well as octopuses, sea otters, and other crabs. Salmon and other finned fish feed on them as larvae.

Commercial harvest began in the mid-1800s in the San Francisco Bay. Today the haul is nearly forty million pounds. The crabs are most commonly caught in steel traps called pots, which are baited with smelly gobs of fish heads, sardines, or even cat food. But there are other ways to skin a crab.

A while back, when my friend Ivar (no connection to Seattle's legendary "acres of clams" chowder magnate) flew in from Boston for a wedding, he asked if he might join me on a crabbing expedition. Ivar really wanted to eat some fresh crab while in town, and he knew I had some opinions on the subject.

My approach to this time-honored Puget Sound ritual is a little different from most. For one thing, I don't use a crab pot. We pulled into the dive shop in Mukilteo so Ivar could rent a wetsuit.

"You're joking, right?"

Not in the least. I suppose it might be easier to paddle a little inflatable raft a hundred yards offshore and drop a pot, but the chase for me is half the fun, maybe more than half. Catching my own food in the wild, if only occasionally, feels like a reasonable response to the mind-numbing chore of pushing a shopping cart down the fluorescent-lit runways of a supermarket.

I tried to explain this to Ivar. We sat in the car and I told him about my first dive in pursuit of crab. It was a wild, exhausting swim in the Sound (I didn't mention the "exhausting" part) as I stalked the crabs through waving pastures of eelgrass near Golden Gardens beach in Seattle. The crabs scuttled, paddled, and otherwise skedaddled with remarkable alacrity when pursued, using their legs like flippers to effect their characteristic sideways scrambles to safety. I cruised the surface looking for them, sometimes diving and swimming along the bottom, where there was less resistance and the freedom of the dive was held back only by the need for air. Crabs on the run disappeared into cloudy blooms of sand.

The best way to catch them, I painfully discovered through trial and error, was to chase them down like a seal, pin them against the bottom, and then carefully, out of reach of the flexing pincers, grab their hind legs. Even if the crabber is wearing a heavy neoprene glove, bigger males can inflict grievous retribution on a wayward pinky, sometimes even slicing through the glove completely to draw blood.

Sitting in the front seat, I carefully explained my methods to Ivar. I had learned a lot on these initial crab dives, and now I wanted to share my knowledge with an eager pupil. Our friend Karl was with us, too, in the backseat. Karl works with sea mammals at the Monterey Bay Aquarium, swimming with injured seals and helping to rehabilitate them back into the wild. Karl's last name is Mayer; he's been known as "Air" Mayer for as long as I've known him, for his habit of jumping off tall things. I once followed Karl seventy vertical feet over a waterfall into a chilly canyon pool, in perhaps one of the stupidest stunts of my life. In the salt he can dive deeper and stay under longer than just about anyone I know.

Ivar turned in his seat, pointing an accusatory finger at Karl. "You were in on this all along."

In the shop we looked through the suits without luck. Ivar is a large man. He played tackle on our college football team back east. I remember seeing a photograph of him taken for the school newspaper. In the picture Ivar is going over the top of a dogpile and looking straight at the camera lens. His arms are spread, hands ready to throttle the quarterback. His face looks like something out of a Halloween drive-in movie. It's a jarring picture: a man transformed into a wild, uncontrollable beast. Ivar's biceps are about the size of my thighs.

Mumbling, the shop clerk disappeared into the back, then reemerged with an extra-extra-large. After what seemed like a long time my friend came out of the dressing room, grousing about the tight fit. "It doesn't feel right," he said, more like a little boy.

"Yeah, but you look good." Karl slapped him on the back. It

was true. All that bulk stuffed inside a tight blue neoprene casing made his muscles stand out even more than usual. Ivar looked like a superhero.

"What you need is a cape."

"It's really hot in here," Ivar complained.

Karl started to laugh. "No wonder, you big dummy. It's inside out."

Somehow Ivar had managed to put the suit on inside out and zip himself up by pulling the leash attached to the zipper. Now he was squeezed in so tight he couldn't get it undone. A look of panic crossed his face. Little beads of sweat were already forming on his forehead. He flailed his arms, trying to reach the zipper.

The three of us stood there in the shop, unsure of what to do next. Finally, Ivar broke the silence. "I'm freaking out. Get me a knife!"

Before Ivar could summon his gridiron strength to burst free, Incredible Hulk-style, we managed to wrestle the zipper down his neck and peel off the suit. He popped out with an audible sigh and wiped the sweat off his brow. "Whose idea was this?" he asked diffidently. "Can't we just buy some crab at the market like normal people?"

Then the clerk came back with the shop's lone triple-X, and we were off. The day was warming up, and we were ready to fall into the Sound's cool arms. Certainly Ivar was. His face was still red, and the sweat from his ordeal showed through his shirt.

We drove past the ferry dock and found a dirt access road that paralleled the railroad tracks. At the end of the road was a gravel parking lot. The tide was still out, and a few Vietnamese families were on the mudflats with buckets and rakes, digging clams. I had dug clams here, too, but recent shellfish advisories now discouraged against it. Soon this beach, like so many others within the clutches of the greater Seattle-Tacoma metro area, would be permanently closed to such activity. Our quarry today, however, moved in from deeper, cleaner waters to breed.

Even in a triple-extra-large wetsuit, Ivar felt squeezed and out of sorts. He walked down to the water with his arms sticking out at an odd angle. Putting on his fins took immense effort, as it involved bending and stretching the taut, elastic suit. I showed him how to spit in his mask and wash it out, but the mask quickly fogged anyway. He floated on his back in the water with his mask off, letting the refreshing sensation of the Sound pour into every nook and cranny.

"I think I'll just stay like this for a while."

"Put your face in the water," Karl commanded. "Use your snorkel." But Ivar didn't want to move. Finally he rolled over and did a dead man's float for a moment before popping up like a wounded seal. "It's claustrophobic in here. I feel like I'm made out of rubber."

Karl shook his head and swam out past the ferry dock while I tried to lead Ivar along the jetty, where it was shallow. Somehow water kept gushing into his mask, and he had to stop and readjust it. He drank a mouthful of the Sound. "Blow out like this," I said, spraying water from my snorkel. Ivar put his face in the water and blew.

"Maybe this wasn't such a good idea. I could always watch from the beach."

"Forget it. We need three limits of crabs. You're in."

After pointing out a few crabs, I encouraged Ivar to catch one. Diving for crabs in the mating season is like shooting tuna in a can, I told him. The males are preoccupied with finding females; they're out on the prowl and vulnerable. Ivar went under tentatively and came up with a snort, spitting water and bobbling a male Dungeness in his hands like a hot potato. The crab was trying to grab his fingers, and Ivar didn't know what to do. Keeping it bouncing in the air must have seemed like a good idea at the time. Both crab and captor waved their appendages madly, and if crabs can talk I'm sure this one was swearing like a sailor, just like Ivar.

I swam over and put the crab in my mesh bag. Ivar let out a shout, something between a whoop and a war cry, as if he had just clotheslined a running back at midfield. Farther out, we could see Karl diving like a porpoise and coming up minutes later with enormous crabs in each hand.

That night our friend John-O was having his wedding rehearsal and dinner at a swank downtown restaurant. Smartly, he'd neglected to invite any of us. Instead, we threw our own party at my place on Capitol Hill. Word must have leaked out, because the house was packed. Though my friends didn't know it yet, this was something of a last hurrah for me too. After renting a string of apartments and shared houses over the years, I would give up my bachelor ways at the end of the month to move in with Martha.

Ivar ran into the kitchen and called for more crabs. Our limit of eighteen seemed suddenly thin. Luckily I had a bunch more in the freezer from previous dives. To make the spoils go further, I started frying up crab cakes in the galley. Marty volunteered her sous chef services, as did our friend Emily, and we soon had the assembly line humming: Marty working a red-hot frying pan to sauté up veggies and Emily flipping the cakes, while I extracted crabmeat and threw together patties with whatever seasonings and condiments I could find. Even when the keg was kicked and Emily had finally relinquished her apron for a cool-down smoke outside, Marty and I were still taking orders, throwing big pads of butter in the sizzling pan and gobbing in patties of my signature cakes.

At last, when each and every finger-nicking shell had been exhumed and the final batch was plated, I came out of the hot kitchen. It was late. Music blared and the living room overflowed with bodies in motion. Ivar and Karl were in a corner, regaling the same girl with increasingly heroic and danger-filled tales of their afternoon dive. The smell of cooked crab hovered in the air like a heavy, sweet fog. Though the beer was gone, there were new faces, fancy outfits, and expensive champagne all around. The wedding party had heard the news: a crab feed was on.

DUNGENESS CRAB CAKES

Cooking crab cakes should become quick and second nature after a couple of tries, and they're always a crowd-pleaser. The key to good crab cakes is a lot of crab. This may sound obvious, but if you've ever ordered them in a restaurant, even some fancy high-end joint, you know that chefs try to stretch their expensive crabmeat as far as possible by adding copious, often distracting fillers—one more reason to make your own.

That said, I like to experiment with different cake recipes to play with the flavor accents and consistency. Such experimenting, it should be noted, is far more economical when not paying fish-market prices. A solid presentation goes something like this.

½ cup diced onion
¼ cup diced red pepper
2 tablespoons butter, divided
Freshly ground black pepper to taste
1 pound Dungeness crabmeat
2 heaping tablespoons chopped fresh parsley
1 large egg, beaten
½ cup quality bread crumbs, or more to taste
1 tablespoon fresh lemon juice
2 teaspoons Old Bay seasoning (optional)
1–2 tablespoons mayonnaise or Dijon mustard (optional)
1 tablespoon Worcestershire sauce (optional)
Lemon wedges for garnish

Sauté onion and red pepper in 2 tablespoons of butter. Add salt and black pepper to taste. In a mixing bowl, combine sautéed vegetables with crabmeat, parsley, egg, bread crumbs, lemon juice, and Old Bay seasoning. Add bread crumbs to taste, not all at once. If desired, add mayo or mustard and Worcestershire sauce. Go wild with the seasonings if you choose—with all the rubs and spice blends on the market these days, the sky's the limit. I stick with Old Bay. Also, additional bread crumbs can be used for dredging if preferred.

Next, form the patties. For firm patties, refrigerate for an hour or so on waxed paper, a step I usually omit due to the flying-by-the-seat-of-my-pants nature of my average crab feed. Then pan-fry in the remaining butter. Make sure you get a nice golden brown crust on the outside to contrast with the succulent inside. **SERVES 4**

SILVER BEACH

IN AUGUST, WITHOUT any sort of gainful employment to
speak of—and with little desire to find any—I gave myself over
to the salt. I had always been a trout man, but now with the extra
time I decided I would get serious about salmon. Each morning
I drove "to work" across the bridge, to a city park with a long
stretch of public beach. The drive felt like a commute. I had my
to-go mug of coffee and an English muffin wrapped in a paper
napkin. I listened to the morning news on the radio.

Even at first light, the park was busy. Couples mooned about
holding hands, pointing at seals in the surf as if they were the
first humans to ever make contact with the animals. Mothers
strolled fussing babes. Joggers, bikers, and Rollerbladers per-
formed their daily routines in bright, efficient Lycra. I had my
own ritual: I made sure to park in a four-hour zone, then sat on
the tailgate to gather my things—rod and reel, a stray collection
of lures that rolled noisily about in the trunk, a water bottle, and
sometimes even a newspaper for those frequent interludes when
nothing much was happening and the idea that something might
happen in the future seemed unlikely at best.

I tried to appear inconspicuous, hurrying down the path in
my waders, the studs on my boots going clack-clack-clack on
the pavement, looking away from the power walkers to scan
the tide for clues—for flocks of birds and the telltale splashes

of little fish being pursued by big fish—but there was always someone who noticed my getup and needed confirmation. "Gonna get one today?" Raising my eyes, I'd try to say something hopeful. "You bet."

Just past the point, I joined a group of mostly elderly men on the beach, men much older than me. I might as well have been stooped over a metal detector. I had my lunch in a brown paper sack like a pensioner. Together we formed a sort of line—railposts silhouetted against the sky—and cast our lots out into the unfathomable water.

This was the season when the silvers run. Each year, as the summer comes to a close, the silver salmon—known variously as coho, hooknoses, or bluebacks, and by the Latin name *Oncorhynchus kisutch*—return from their mysterious sojourns at sea, leaving hunting grounds in the North Pacific where they've fattened up for a couple years in preparation for grueling spawning runs up the coastal rivers. The schools funnel into the Sound and feed voraciously in a last bid for upstream fuel. Though not quite as revered as the larger, meatier chinooks, or king salmon, the silvers still have the firm, bright red flesh of a good eating salmon—and they fight, I was told, like caged tigers.

The beach scene appealed to me. There was a sense of camaraderie. We celebrated each other's catches. Landing an eight-pound silver meant food for a week for some lucky angler. As I glanced around, I had to conclude that many of these fishermen, like me, weren't looking too hard for work. These were my people.

In the mornings, while it was still dark outside, I would be stepping into my waders while Martha was pulling on her pantyhose and telling me how she was late, how she needed to beat the traffic. I couldn't disagree with that logic. She'd have a list of chores for me before going out the door. I was becoming a very efficient dish loader. I knew the washer and dryer on a first-name basis. Just before the front door closed, there'd be a pause: "Are we having salmon tonight?"

You bet.

Later, in the evenings, after I heard the turn of the lock and watched Martha come into the kitchen with her shoulder bag already landing in the middle of the floor as she reached for an uncorked bottle of wine—with a slightly ironic "Did you have a good day?"—I'd explain that salmon was not yet the house special, but soon. Soon.

Part of the problem was that I was using a little spinning rod I'd found in the basement. It seemed a bit extravagant to me—a man with no job—to go out and buy a new rod so I could go fishing instead of looking for work. Besides, I liked to think I was putting food on the table without spending a dime. The only thing was, I wasn't. And the few fish I hooked kept shaking off.

This sad state of affairs wasn't missed by the regulars on the beach. One morning, after watching me lose a nice silver, one of them sauntered over while I battled another, a cigarette dangling from her lip as she looked on. My plastic reel groaned under the pressure, and the rod whipsawed back and forth. "Keep the tip up," she admonished, pointing her Camel Light at me like a professor's ruler. I had the fish in the shallows now and could see it was a beauty, big and glinting with a tail like a garden spade. A few more regulars interrupted their casting to come over and offer moral support.

I was thinking about what this slab-sided fish would look like on the grill—bright red flesh gleaming with olive oil and dotted with a few green sprigs of rosemary and white grinds of garlic, how Martha would be beside herself—when I heard a pop and nearly fell over backward. My lure flew out of the water like a slingshot and whistled past my ear. The salmon, half out of the surf, kicked its massive tail once and vanished back into the waves.

"Shoulda kept your tip up."

The anticlimax was palpable. Everyone went back to what they were doing, with eyes averted to save me the embarrassment of consolation. I packed up my things and drove directly to my neighborhood tackle shop, a place of dusty shelves and little commerce. "I need a respectable salmon rod," I told the clerk behind the counter, a diminutive Filipino woman of advanced age. I showed her what I had been using.

"That's cheapo trout rod. You no land salmon on that thing." She shook her head in disgust. I was sullying the place as I stood there.

"I know, I know."

"Here, you want this." She put a salmon rod in my hand. It was a good three feet longer than my other rod. "Feel this." She grabbed the tip and bent the rod over double, imitating the action of a heavy-bodied fish. "No problem, right?" She stroked the rod with a wrinkled finger right along the butt section. "What you need is backbone."

I said I'd take it. She matched the rod with a reel and wound twelve-pound test on it. I bought a handful of lures and a small tackle box to hold them.

The regulars at the beach admired my new setup. Only $50, I crowed. There was Cheri, the day-trading, chain-smoking den mother of the gang, and her husband; a couple of local firefighters who fished whenever they weren't at the station; several retirees who spent their days at the beach, mostly playing cards at a picnic table; Sunny, with his graying dreadlocks and flip-flops and a distinctly warm disposition; an old Indian-looking guy with a shark-tooth necklace and a Panama hat; and a hunched eighty-year-old Chinese man named Louie, who always caught the biggest fish.

The old guys especially seemed to have latched on to some hard-won wisdom over the years. They weren't in a hurry. When one of them caught a fish, they all admired it for a while on the beach. One that got off was easy come, easy go. It occurred to me that they had caught a lot of fish over the years, more than I would ever know. The regulars were there nearly every day—and then there was Trouthole.

One morning I arrived to find an old colleague of mine string-
ing up his flyrod. Trouthole—that's his *nom de plume*—eyed me
suspiciously.

"What are you doing here? It's 8:00 AM on a Tuesday."

"I could ask you the same."

"Working," he said. "Putting food on the table."

"Me too."

In an earlier life, Trouthole and I had worked together at
the same company, though on different "teams." As these things
go, we discovered we had a mutual interest in trout fishing and
started making trips together. Our go-to water was a curvy, canyon stretch of river on the east side of the mountains, where
native redsides—a type of desert-dwelling rainbow trout—made
for good sport on light flyrods. In fall, when the cottonwoods
turned yellow, we camped down by the water's edge and fished
from morning until dark.

The day Trouthole became my boss was a dark one. I arrived
that morning to find that many of our colleagues were being
sacked as the company, newly public, bowed to Wall Street pressure to cut costs. Trouthole got a promotion.

"You've still got a job with my team," he said to me, "if you
want it."

"Let me think about it."

"Not much to think about. You work for me or pack your
things."

The arrangement didn't turn out to be as awkward as I'd
feared, and we still fished for trout on occasion. When I gave
notice a few years later, he actually seemed sad—this despite
his toast at my birthday luncheon, when he declared me
"unbossable."

Like me, Trouthole had fled the corporate world and was
now unemployed. He looked at my new spinning rod. "What's
up with the ugly stick?"

"I'm not one of those fly-fishing purists."

"No kidding."

"This is about getting dinner. I'm not ashamed." I unhooked my Buzzbomb from the hook-keeper, an unartful hunk of lead painted hot pink, and let it sail thirty yards out into the chop. Trouthole snorted and stepped into the water. He stripped some line off, then double-hauled and landed his fly about eighty feet out. "Look at that. Nothing gives me more pleasure than casting just as far as you hardware boys. Five bucks says I'll catch a fish before you."

"I'd rather not demean our ancient pastime."

"Beers at the local. I'll give you 2-1 odds."

Before I could reject his overture, Trouthole was into a fish. He fought it to the surfline and then horsed his salmon up onto the beach in front of a crowd of tourists. Kneeling beside it, he looked up at me and grinned, then turned gravely to the crowd closing in for a look. "This," he said, reaching theatrically for the nearest stone of consequence, "is called the rock shampoo."

One afternoon I got to the beach late and had to take my place at the end of the line, far from the point and, I was sure, far from the sweet spot. The day was windy, with uncharacteristically large waves crashing on the cobbles. It was Sunday and few of the regulars were around, just a bunch of weekend warriors tossing their lures out and hardly bothering to reel them back in. They didn't expect to catch anything; I could see that right away. They were hiding from chores and honey-do lists. It occurred to me that I was just about the only regular in attendance, if I could be so bold as to call myself that.

Just then I saw an interesting sight through my polarized lenses: plain as day, a pod of silvers zipped by in the curl of a wave mere yards offshore, fin to fin like a squadron of Blue Angels in tight formation. I looked at the guy next me. Am I seeing things? He couldn't summon much energy and robotically cast his line way over the salmon, fifty yards out to sea (this was better than painting the garage, that's for sure). A few minutes later and the squadron was back. I put my lure in front of the pod, just a few yards out. A fish peeled off the group and hammered it in less than a foot of water. Seconds later, I had a six-pound silver on the beach.

The guy next to me was surprised. "Wow, you got one," he said, as if we were all assembled there for some obscure reason that had yet to be revealed. Five minutes later and I had my second. A limit. Silver salmon was on the menu at last.

People have fished for salmon in this area for hundreds, even thousands of years. Before the first Europeans settled in 1851, just around the corner at a place they optimistically called New York-*Alki* (in the local Salish tongue "New York by-and-by"), native tribes prospered from the fecundity of Puget Sound. They speared salmon and corralled them into nets; they lashed together weirs from willow sticks and secured them in shallow sections of river, then used dip nets to scoop up the fish where they collected.

The Puget Sound Indians were so good at fishing, in fact, that they had to create elaborate rituals to ensure that the salmon spirits were properly appeased and the resource not overexploited. In their annual First Salmon Ceremony, they offered their respects at the beginning of the run to the Salmon People, who sent their ambassadors up the rivers each year to nourish the tribes. The first salmon was captured and brought to the village as an honored guest, where it was ritualistically prepared and eaten by all members of the community. The tribe hoped the salmon would feel welcome and well treated and would return again. The skeleton of the first salmon was then floated back downriver so it could receive a dignified burial and reincarnation.

These were the descendants of the first immigrants to North America, the Paleolithic hunter-gatherers who crossed the Bering land bridge 20,000 to 10,000 years ago in search of new hunting grounds, the brave souls who weathered terrible storms and skirted enormous walls of ice—some of them a mile high—while migrating into the newly opened valleys where retreating glaciers promoted an abundance of game and fish. Can we even imagine how giving the land was back then?

Nonetheless, early explorers looked down on the coastal Indians. These were not the noble warriors of the plains. Some of them were even fat! They ate deer, elk, seals, ducks, shellfish, huckleberries, camas bulbs, and plenty more. But more than anything else, these people were nourished and defined by the great runs of salmon, which they smoked and sun-dried for use throughout the year.

By 1855, only a few years after the first white settlers had arrived on the shores of Puget Sound, the native population had an inkling of the future. Representatives from eighty-one local tribes signed the Point Elliott Treaty, ceding territory to the newly arrived whites in exchange for cash and rights to their historic hunting and fishing grounds. As long as they could continue to hunt and fish in their "usual and accustomed places," they figured they'd be okay. But the salmon runs would never be the same. In 1877 the first cannery was built in the area, at Mukilteo. By 1899, canneries in the Puget Sound were packing nearly a million cases of salmon annually. Then the runs crashed and various government agencies stepped in, constructing fish hatcheries to mitigate the loss of wild salmon to development and overfishing, failing to understand truths that any third-grader could grasp. Now the salmon runs are a tiny fraction of their historical size. A famous court case in 1974 known as the Boldt Decision—named for the federal judge who presided, George Boldt—reaffirmed the right of Native Americans to take half of Washington's salmon harvest. The rest is split between recreational and commercial anglers. Though the tribes and the state have been co-managing salmon populations since the Boldt Decision, some runs have gone extinct, while others are barely hanging on. The silvers remain listed under the Endangered Species Act as a species "of concern." Each year, anglers hope to hear from the biologists at Fish and Wildlife that numbers are up, with an outlook for fabulous fishing on the horizon, and each year they're disappointed. Still, we go to our chosen spots and hope to get lucky.

A rumor was circulating at the beach. Someone had hooked and landed a funny-looking salmon the other day. Something about it didn't seem right. One of the regulars knew what it was, though: an escapee, he called it, an Atlantic salmon that had gotten loose from one of the salmon farming operations. This was a bad omen. The farmed salmon, almost always Atlantics, frequently escape from their confinement to wreak havoc on native stocks. They spread disease and compete for spawning habitat. Wherever salmon farming has flourished around the world, the political will to support wild salmon has disappeared—and with it the wild salmon themselves.

When I was young, it was a tradition in our family to visit my grandparents on Cape Cod for the Fourth of July and eat an Atlantic salmon dinner. The light pink meat, usually poached or broiled, didn't appeal to me, so I slathered it with Hollandaise sauce and choked down what I could. This was well before consumers began questioning the wisdom of farmed fish, and I suppose it didn't occur to me that salmon need not be mushy and weak-tasting. Farm-raised Atlantic salmon were a fact of life in New England and elsewhere on both sides of the Atlantic; their wild counterparts were nearly extinct in most of their range.

Not until I moved to Seattle did I realize what I was missing. Each spring, the city's food lovers begin anticipating the arrival of the first Pacific salmon runs of the year. These Columbia River spring chinook, known as "springers" or "upriver brights," are the same fish that many Indian tribes welcomed in their First Salmon ceremonies, and they arrive in the fish markets with fanfare.

Eating one grilled at a backyard barbecue, I realized the farmed salmon I'd grown up with was a complete imposter. These fillets were deep red and firm. You could grill them like steaks and not worry about the meat going to pieces with an errant flip of the spatula. After the spring chinook, fishmongers sell troll-caught salmon from up and down the West Coast, and then in May and June the renowned Alaskan runs start coming in by plane: Copper River sockeye and Yukon chinook, to name a couple.

Chefs prize the fish from the coldest, swiftest rivers. These hardy salmon require more fat reserves to ascend to their spawning grounds, the fat translating into flavor. Nutritionists extol the salubrious virtues of omega-3 fatty acids. And, as home cooks and backyard barbecue enthusiasts will be delighted to discover, wild salmon fillets are nearly impervious to rookie culinary mistakes. Marinated or with a dry rub, barbecued salmon fillets are one of the great treats of summer. The key is making sure the fish aren't farmed. Farmed salmon are raised in floating net-pens and fattened on fishmeal laced with antibiotics. The pens keep predators at bay, allowing the salmon to live idle lives of complacency. Because of their unnatural diets, farmed salmon have dull gray flesh and require special dyes to acquire the more palatable pink coloring that consumers expect. Seattle fish markets are always careful to advertise the difference, but in places on the East Coast that long ago lost their wild salmon, unscrupulous fishmongers have been caught trying to market farmed salmon as wild. The deception can go only so far: discerning palates will usually recognize the insipid flavor and texture of farmed Atlantic salmon.

While Alaska has banned salmon farming in its state waters to protect native fish, British Columbia and Washington State continue to experiment with farming. My neighbor, a food consultant working on various political issues related to organic and local food—like getting locally produced vegetables into public schools—says salmon farming is a loaded gun waiting to go off, and before we know what hit us it'll be too late, as the farms proliferate and wild runs go in the toilet. "Farmed and Dangerous," reads the bumper sticker on her car.

I asked Kristin whether it was ethically okay that I was fishing for salmon, never mind that it was legal. She said the worst thing that could happen to salmon was lack of interest among anglers. "They're as good as extinct at that point," she said. "Anglers and commercial fishermen need to keep fishing—and demanding that their legislators take the necessary steps to protect ocean and river conditions."

By September I'd caught enough silvers to start stocking the freezer with fillets. My newfound success also had the odd (especially to Martha's thinking) effect of stalling any sort of job search whatsoever, since now I was determined to take my mastery to the next level. I called up Trouthole.

"Hey, Boss."

"Don't call me that."

"Any fish around?"

"Maybe."

Trouthole was raised in Detroit. His father worked at the ultimate blue-collar firm, the Ford Motor Company, and though he was management, Trouthole grew up with a rivet-head's range of betrayable emotions. A colleague of ours once referred to him as "rectangular shaped." The description is apt. Trouthole gambles and plays ice hockey. He likes good scotch. Jim Harrison is his hero. In case of emergency, he keeps a .44 in a drawer.

"Catch any lately?"

"Perhaps."

"Is this going to be a game of Magic 8-Ball, or are you going to emit a few more syllables?"

"The outlook is good."

"I've got a flyrod. When should I come over?"

"Tomorrow morning, before slack."

An hour before low tide, I pulled up in front of Trouthole's home. The house gave off a whiff of the college dorm. One bedroom was devoted to his instruments—guitars and amps and such. Empty bottles lined the windowsill behind the living room couch. The place smelled of cigarettes and stale beer. Cards littered the kitchen table.

"You should have been here ten hours ago," he yawned. "I made eighty clams."

"Where's Red?"

"Business trip. Keeping this whole enterprise afloat." After years of saying he would never marry, Trouthole had recently asked for the hand of an auburn beauty ten years his junior who was known, on camping trips, to twirl flaming batons around her head in a midnight fire dance for the Burning Man set. I witnessed the wedding myself. Red came down the aisle to the unmistakable twang of "I Walk the Line," and later, at the reception, she joined a fiddle-violin combo to sing a rowdy version of "Folsom Prison Blues."

We went from room to room, gathering up his gear. I was glad to see he had finally trimmed back the muttonchops. Since leaving the company he had been working on a novel, a sort of historical fish fantasy set during the first year of the Lewis and Clark expedition, told from the point of view of the official Corps of Discovery angler-in-chief.

Trouthole had done his homework. He tossed around a lexicon of antiquated frontier language that would make Cormac McCarthy blush. The novel was written entirely in dialect. After reading a few chapters, I suggested that he ease up on the reader just a smidgen and tone down the vernacular, citing (I thought smartly) *Huckleberry Finn* as an example. Trouthole rejected the idea out of hand. There would be no easing up on anybody.

All this immersion in nineteenth-century mores and figures of speech had, of late, taken a physical toll on Trouthole. He was beginning to dress like a sodbuster. Half the time I had no idea what he was saying, and then there were those Stonewall Jackson muttonchops. He could have been an extra in a Civil War movie. He was playing a lot of poker and doing inexplicable things to dead animals in the kitchen. How Red put up with any of this behavior was a mystery. Then again, bringing home fresh salmon fillets every morning by sunup can have a peculiar effect on some wives.

We drove the short distance to the park. On the far side of
the point, several of the regulars were already in attendance,
flinging their lures out into the swells. I strung up an eight-
weight flyrod with a new flyline purchased just for the salt. In
the hands of a flycaster who knows what he's doing, the line
was capable of shooting a hundred feet or more; in my hands, it
might go sixty. I tied on a pink fly with dumbbell eyes. Trouthole
watched me with his rod tucked under one arm. "Think you
have what it takes to operate that thing?"

"We'll see."

"Right quick, I expect."

After a couple of casts I lost my fly on the rocks behind me.
Trouthole diagnosed my problem as a "weak-ass double-haul"
and handed me another fly from the bill of his cap. He demon-
strated the correct technique and dropped his fly into a slick
just beyond a band of fast-moving water, a place where baitfish
can become disoriented and thrown to the mercy of the tide. He
stripped in his fly without event and cast again. An hour passed,
and still nothing.

Normally under slow fishing conditions, Trouthole would
keep up a steady patter of off-color stories and maybe some big
league baseball analysis, but today he seemed uncharacteristically
distracted. After a while the wind came up and Trouthole got discouraged. He said he had some things "to take care of" at home.
I stuck around and wrestled with the wind. No one was catching anything. Then, just past noon, another flycaster tied into a
beautiful fish, maybe nine pounds. It took line and the fisherman worked to get it back. The fish leaped clear of the water
and ran again. This went on for a while until he had it in close
and beached it. The salmon was still gasping for breath when
he whipped out a cell phone and called home to his wife. If
Trouthole had been here, there might have been a fight. I stepped
back in the water and redoubled my resolve. A fish grabbed my
fly and took off. Within seconds it threw the hook. The next fish
wasn't so lucky. This time I was ready and kept him tight on my

line. He ran to the right and then the left. He came toward me and I gathered up the slack. In the shallows he thrashed in a way that reminded me that his biological imperative was being denied, and I pulled him up on the beach. Not huge—maybe four pounds—but silver and hooked in the corner of his mouth on my fly. I waited until I was halfway down the path to the car, my catch cleaned and in a bag, before I got out my phone.

Toward the end of the season, Trouthole stopped showing up at the beach altogether. Recently he had asked me to be a job reference, and he said I might get some calls from prospective employers.

"Don't do it," I pleaded with him. "It'll just be me and a bunch of old guys. Finish the novel first." But he'd made up his mind. At the beach I kept waiting for one of the regulars to ask me why I still wasn't working, but no one asked questions like that. In mid-October Louie, the octogenarian, landed a thirteen-pound silver. Rather than run up the beach and drag the salmon from the water, he played it in the surf, gallantly soaking his loafers and pant cuffs while leading the fish back and forth in the shallows like a dog on a leash until it had exhausted itself. Then he bent over carefully and grabbed it by the gill.

Back on dry land, after dispatching the fish with a piece of driftwood, he stood over it for a while. A couple of other regulars joined him. They circled the salmon, hands clasped behind their backs, staring and nodding. Then Louie went to fetch his knife. Later he came up to me, his eyes just visible behind tinted lenses, his voice barely audible. "I worked all my life," he said matter-of-factly. "Retirement is good." I didn't know what to say to that.

He went on in a low rasp. "These young guys"—as if I might have been a spokesperson for all of them—"they don't know the proper landing technique. You stay in the water with the salmon. If he throws the hook, you can kick him up on shore." This seemed questionable to me, possibly illegal, but how could I contradict someone of Louie's stature?

"How long have you been fishing around here, Louie?"

He gestured with the palm of his hand, holding it about waist-high.

"What was it like back in the day? I know it's a bad question, but I need to know."

"Oh man," he said in a whisper. "We killed 'em. In the Fifties? You wouldn't believe it. We killed 'em." With that he picked up his tackle box and the plastic bag holding his big silver salmon, and strapped first the box and then the bag to his two-wheeled hand-truck with a pair of bungee cords. He stood up and looked around as if he might have forgotten something. "See you tomorrow," he said finally, already moving away, his back turned, choosing his steps carefully as he walked along the beach path toward the distant parking lot, slightly stooped over as always, pulling the hand-truck with the silver behind him.

GRILLED SALMON

Northwest grillmasters jealously guard innumerable secret marinades, rubs, and techniques for grilling their salmon on the barbecue. There are so many decisions to be made. What cut do you use, for instance? The fish can be filleted or sliced into steaks. It can be cooked on a wooden plank. Do you marinate it or give it a rub? One salmon aficionado I know insists on a dry rub of salt, paprika, onion flakes, curry powder, coriander, black pepper, and brown sugar, which he massages into the fillets and drizzles with maple syrup. The truth is, a wild Pacific salmon, unlike a farmed Atlantic, needs little pampering to taste great cooked over coals. Sometimes I just brush on a little olive oil and salt and pepper.

My standby marinade takes about 30 seconds, including the time to rummage through our mixed-up cupboards, and it's particularly effective on fillets that have hidden out in the freezer a bit longer than optimum (more than three months). Place the fillets in a glass dish and brush on 1 part hot chili oil or Mongolian fire oil (a tablespoon for a

1-pound fillet), 2 parts sesame oil, and enough soy sauce to bathe the fish, which is now turned skin up. Minced garlic and ginger add zest— and a few extra minutes of prep time. I like to marinate for a couple of hours in the fridge if possible.

Such a marinade encourages a pan-Asian presentation. *My usual sides are julienned vegetables—zucchini, squash, onions—sautéed in the same marinade, and jasmine rice or couscous; a salsa of diced red pepper, red onion, mango, and cilantro also pairs nicely. For a more French or American flavor, I usually stick with a simple olive oil and chopped rosemary solution, brushed on with salt and pepper right on the grill, although my friend Bradley makes a terrific traditional dill sauce with a lot of mayo, dried or fresh dill, lemon juice, and cored and chopped cucumber. Whatever you do, don't ape the glossy magazine photos and cover your salmon with sliced lemons—unless you plan to eat ceviche.*

OF BEARS AND BERRY EATERS

A CENTURY AGO, young people went huckleberrying with the hope of picking more than berries. The huckleberry patch was a place to find respite from the workaday world, to find fun and adventure. It was also a place to go in search of romance. Think about it. While out picking berries all day, there isn't much else to do but keep up your end of the conversation with whomever is nearby. Or maybe duck down into the bushes with someone. In the Northwest, extended clans of both whites and Indians spent weeks in summer camping out in the legendary patches: in what is now Glacier National Park, in Montana; in the Blue Mountains of northeastern Oregon; and all over the volcanic triangle of Washington State between Mounts Adams, St. Helens, and Rainier, especially on the high plateau that is now the Indian Heaven Wilderness.

Indian Heaven, known to the Yakama and Klickitat Indians as Sahalee Tyee, is a place of seismic upheaval and spent cinder cones. The rolling plateau left behind by lava flows is a snow trap in winter and a spongelike receptacle for meltwater in summer— in other words, a Mosquito Heaven. Martha and I made our way on a tough dirt track from the north, skirting designated wilderness along the flanks of Sawtooth Mountain and a three-mile stretch called the Berry Grounds.

A wooden sign on the east side of the road laid out the

terms: "The Handshake Agreement of 1932 reserves the picking of huckleberries on this side of road for Indians." A few folks wearing improvised milk jugs around their necks to carry the berries worked the exposed patches near the road, but most of the action was to the south, in lower-elevation patches closer to Petersen Prairie and Trout Lake. The winter had been long and hard, and significant drifts of dirty snow still held on like bad rashes in the gullies and clefts of the wilderness. Tenacious little mosquitoes and larger deerflies exacted a hefty toll from anyone stepping outside the safety of their tent.

Yet it was a toll we were willing to pay. Here, where abject conditions of snow, volcanic ash, and fire-swept forests had converged for thousands of years, the huckleberry bushes responded as if in angry defiance, with enormous purple fruits rivaling in size the hybrid domesticated blueberries you can find in the market these days. But the huckleberry is wild, and its complex flavor of sucrose and tang reminds you of the lengths taken to secure its promise. No wonder bands of Indians gathered here every summer to hunt, fish, pick berries, race horses, and play games. Hanging around Indian Heaven is like working in a confectionary.

Of course, we're not the only mammals that see it this way.

Spend enough time tramping around the woods, and sooner or later you'll meet an animal larger, stronger, and fouler-smelling than yourself—and it won't be an herbivore. Happily, the critter I'm thinking of won't be a carnivore either, strictly speaking. Like you and me, it will be an omnivore, an animal with a broad, adaptable palate, and for that we can be thankful, because nuts and berries are far safer forage for an omnivore than meat, especially living meat. Then again, you might find yourself gathering the same berries that our hirsute friend considers his, which is when things can get interesting.

Bears and berries go together. We might as well accept that. Bears crave fattening sweets just like us, and if you're given to gathering berries outside of town, there's a good chance you'll happen on a bear at some point. I know an elderly lady who was picking blackberries in Oregon's coastal mountains. As she worked her way deeper into a huge thicket that towered over her head, she became aware of another picker in the patch. Carefully she pulled back a thorny branch to eyeball her competition— revealing an equally curious black nose inches from her own. Both parties bolted headlong in opposite directions.

That's how most bear encounters usually end. More often than not you won't see the bear at all. Martha and I were camping in the Blue Mountains a few summers ago, in a place geology forgot near the headwaters of the Umatilla and Walla Walla rivers, on a scenic subalpine plateau. This was high country, though much of it wasn't steep. The huckleberry patch went on for miles of gentle walking, thriving beneath an open canopy of widely spaced firs and pines.

This gladelike setting was probably the result of fire. We like to think of Native Americans as the original practitioners of "leave no trace" camping, but in fact the Indians manipulated the landscape to their needs. They set fires to clear underbrush and promote habitat for certain species of plants and animals. Now, after more than a century of Smokey Bear and misguided fire management, such open forests are scarce. The Warm Springs tribe in central Oregon, for instance, wants to renew burnings on their ancestral berry-picking grounds of Mount Hood, where the huckleberries have been choked out by competition; for now they must travel north to the far side of the Columbia and the flanks of another volcano, Mount Adams, to practice their age-old craft.

Like the many other campers who had converged on this prime berry-picking spot above the Umatilla, we roamed the patches around our campsite, moving ever deeper into the bush as we picked. Faint trails bobbed and weaved among chest-high bushes. Pickers called to each other through the forest. It was Huckleberry Central. We carried a couple of beach pails in bright colors, while the serious pickers sported gallon jugs and buckets

hanging from lanyards around their necks so they could pick
with both hands.

These were mostly family operations, extended groups vaca-
tioning together to pick enough berries in the national forest to
last the year. They camped in RVs and even the smallest children
joined in, which amazed me. The work is backbreaking not in
its strenuousness but in its repetitiveness. It requires an attention
span you wouldn't expect from a nine-year-old, and certainly not
from a teenager. Though special combs that can sieve a dozen or
more berries from their branch make the work more efficient, the
digital dexterity required to handle so many berries is still considerable, and unlike mushroom hunting, progress through the
woods can be slow. We heard the older folks urging on their kids
with contests and similar inducements, and the ploys seemed
to work. These people were taking home gallons. "We did two
dozen last weekend," a long-haired boy of about thirteen told
me. His grandmother would make jams, jellies, and syrups and
put up the rest in vacuum-sealed bags in the freezer.

Marty and I weren't quite so ambitious. We wanted enough
to make a pie and a couple of cobblers—still a good 20 cups'
worth. The idea of having a few extra bags in the freezer for
compotes and sauces seemed worth the threat of carpal tunnel
syndrome, too. Yet these few quarts took longer to gather than I
care to admit.

We followed a game trail and picked on either side. Someone
had tied flags of fluorescent surveyor's tape every twenty-five
yards or so to mark their path. A quarter mile into the forest we
came to an opening. The plateau gave way to a canyon, and we
could see down into a river valley below. Bushwhacking down
into the canyon looked like an impossible chore, with a steep
slope covered in brush.

The view was a complete surprise, and for a moment, standing there in filtered light at the edge of a precipice, we felt like
the first explorers in unmapped territory, as if we had stepped
into one of those nineteenth-century American landscape

OF BEARS AND BERRY EATERS   163

paintings depicting the westward discovery of the continent. I almost wanted to hold up my arm and point, never mind the substitution of synthetics for buckskins.

The illusion was popped by a deep voice behind us. "Right where you're standing," said the voice, startling us out of our historical moment. We turned to see an elderly man in red suspenders with a jug of huckleberries. He sat on a stump as if rooted there, with no intention of moving for quite some time. We waved our pails in a huckleberry salute.

"Turned tail and scrambled down yonder into that mess."

"Who's that?"

"Not who but what. Why, the bear you just scared up. Ran past me and down the hill like it was nothing at all."

"The bear?"

"Look at your feet."

We looked down. All around were great piles of dark, berry-filled bear scat, mounds of it.

Occasionally a bear encounter involves a less apparition-like bear. A friend of mine in Vermont was camping under the stars and woke up his buddies in the middle of the night. He was talking in his sleep, calling out his girlfriend's name. Someone shone a flashlight in his direction, boot at the ready, and illuminated a young bear giving my friend a wet willy. The bear took off when confronted, but not before cleaning the pots and pans—and my friend's obviously unscrubbed face. That was a bear that, unfortunately, had been habituated to humans, and it wasn't the standard-issue hurled boots and clapping of the campers that scared it away; it was the howls of mortification from my friend when he awoke to a hairy beast that was decidedly not the girlfriend he had been dreaming about.

Berry pickers—and just about everyone else who spends time in the outdoors, for that matter—are a little more cautious in the Northern Rockies. The common black bear (*Ursus americanus*) may seem like an overgrown Lab much of the time to those familiar with bear country, but the grizzly (*Ursus arctos horribilis*), as well as being another species, is another kettle of fish altogether. Foragers in Montana, Wyoming, and western Canada know this. (Supposedly a few grizzlies are running around in the North Cascades too, though I've never seen one in Washington.) The true outdoorsman, who recognizes the right of all living things to do their own thing within the web of life, can take whatever solace he can find in Doug Peacock's great aphorism of the wild: "It ain't wilderness unless there's a critter out there that can kill you and eat you."

That's cold comfort in your sleeping bag at night.

Foragers know they have more to fear from a lightning storm, a bad clam, or getting lost in the woods. Heck, statistically the drive is more challenging to your health than any interaction with nature. But that doesn't change what my friend Bradley calls the reptilian brain effect—the response from the most primitive part of our cerebral cortex, which manages fear. Walking a trail after dark—or, worse, bushwhacking at night—is license for the imagination to run wild. Sounds beyond the arc of a headlamp are magnified; the snap of a twig insinuates a giant paw. Under such conditions *the idea* of bear takes over—from the lumbering gait to the gaping, halitosis-besotted maw—resulting in the most obvious output of the reptilian brain: the hair on the back of your neck stands on end.

The frequent forager knows better somewhere in the more modern folds of gray matter, but this doesn't mean he might not still surprise Mr. Bear out on the hustings. Usually such encounters go the way of my own inaugural experience trick-or-treating on Halloween, when, seeing my ghostly, bedsheet-bedecked reflection in the door glass of the very first house, I turned heel and ran.

Still, it's something to think about. The mountain huckleberry is the black bear's bonbon of choice around here, and increasingly, it is the forager's too. Huckleberries grow best in damp, acidic soils, which is why the Northwest is such a heavy bearer. Here they thrive on mountain slopes and in open forests. Huckleberries are members of the genus *Vaccinium*, along with blueberries, bilberries, cranberries, and a host of oddly named berries including crowberries, cowberries, whortleberries, farkleberries, and sparkleberries. They can be either deciduous or evergreen. Commercial blueberries are native to eastern North America and include primarily the lowbush, highbush, and rabbiteye varieties.

Huckleberries are strictly wild and can be distinguished from their more domesticated relative by a tarter taste and larger, harder seeds. While this seediness has made the blueberry the chosen berry for commercial cultivation, for some it is the tartness of the huckleberry that makes all the difference. A huckleberry pie or cobbler has that perfect balance of pucker and sweetness that makes it the favorite dessert of many a westerner. Not surprisingly, huckleberry hounds will go to ungodly lengths to satisfy this craving—even driving five hours to a place aptly nicknamed Mosquito Heaven to stock up on the berries. Like their blueberry cousin, huckleberries are valued for their antioxidants. The evergreen huckleberry (*Vaccinium ovatum*) and thinleaf huckleberry (*Vaccinium membranaceum*) are the most well known. New growth on these handsome shrubs is bright red, contrasting with the green leaves. The ripe fruit is a dark blue to purple.

Native Americans in the Northwest picked huckleberries in huge amounts to eat fresh or dry into cakes. They carved combs out of wood or used salmon backbones to harvest the berries more efficiently, then sun-dried and mashed them. The cakes were wrapped in leaves for storage. Lewis and Clark ate huckleberry cakes while visiting with the Shoshone, then directed their camp cook to add flour, resulting in what was perhaps the first huckleberry cobbler, of sorts, as reported by Captain Lewis:

> This morning I arose very early and as hungry as a wolf. I had eaten nothing yesterday except one scant meal of the

flour and berries, except the dried cakes of berries, which did not appear to satisfy my appetite as they appeared to do those of my Indian friends. I found on inquire of McNeal that we had only about two pounds of flour remaining. This I directed him to divide into two equal parts and to cook the one half this morning in a kind of pudding with the berries as he had done yesterday, and reserve the balance for the evening. On this new-fashioned pudding four of us breakfasted, giving a pretty good allowance also to the chief, who declared it the best thing he had tasted for a long time.

Right around this time the Corps of Discovery was also learning just how formidable an opponent the grizzly bear could be, prompting Lewis to write: "I must confess that I do not like the gentlemen and had reather [sic] fight two Indians than one bear."

As for me, my first face-to-face bear encounter was in the Olympic Mountains, and I remember it clearly.

Orange light filled the western sky. Soon it would be dark, the time when big bewhiskered things go scratching around in the night. Martha and I hurried down the trail toward our camp by Heart Lake. In one hand I carried my binoculars, in the other a canteen filled to the brim with a commodity more precious, at that moment, than water. Earlier in the day we had watched golden eagles hunting marmots along the High Divide. We had followed a trail that petered out and then bushwhacked another mile into a forgotten corner of the Olympics known as the Bailey Range. Now, returning to base camp, we had one more reminder of a memorable day spent in the mountains: huckleberries. A full quart of the sweet, tangy globes. Huckleberry pancakes were on the menu for breakfast, and I suppose I was imagining we might get after some of that traditional huckleberry romance after dinner.

We rounded a corner and Martha stopped suddenly. She turned and faced me.

"What you've been waiting for," she said, and pointed.

Maybe seventy-five yards away and just a few feet off the trail was a good-sized bear. A black bear, although at that moment it might as well have been a grizzly for all I knew. I could feel my heart trying to escape out of my rib cage, and though my first instinct was to flee, Marty put a steadying hand on my arm and we watched the bear together.

This bear was browsing huckleberries, just as we had been a short while earlier, and after a staring contest, during which it sniffed the air and determined we were no threat, it went back to browsing. Through binoculars I could see it sift the branches with its long claws like a comb and come away with mouthfuls of ripe berries. The bear was almost human in its systematic approach to each bush. It had little interest in us. Probably we could have continued on down the path and the bear would have taken off for less exposed climes, but we decided to detour above the trail and over the side of a small mountain, arriving back at our campsite by descending the bowl of a cirque on the far side of our tent. From the rim I could still see the bear in the waning light. It was still grazing on the berries, fattening up on as many as possible before the long winter ahead.

BUTTER WORSHIPPER'S HUCKLEBERRY COBBLER

Like blueberries, huckleberries keep well in the freezer. So, unlike a bear, you can indulge a sweet tooth any time of year. A snowy winter evening is an especially good time to surprise your dining companions with a huckleberry cobbler hot out of the oven. Over the years we've tried any number of different cobbler recipes, and yet I always find myself returning to the sort of presentation you might find in a small-town diner. Mark Bittman has codified a similar approach in How to Cook Everything. *If you couldn't care less how many grams of fat are in your dessert (it's dessert, for crissakes!), this is for you.*

4–5 cups huckleberries (or other berries)
1 cup sugar
½ cup flour
½ teaspoon baking powder
Pinch of salt
8 tablespoons (1 stick) cold unsalted butter, cut into small pieces
1 egg
½ teaspoon vanilla extract

Preheat oven to 375 degrees. Toss berries with half the sugar and spread in greased 8-inch square or 9-inch round baking pan. (If using frozen berries, be sure to thaw them first and drain well.) Combine flour, baking powder, salt, and remaining sugar in a bowl. Mix in cold butter pieces with a pastry blender until well blended. By hand, beat in egg and vanilla. Drop mixture on fruit by the spoonful; do not spread. Bake until topping is golden yellow, 35 to 45 minutes. Serve with vanilla ice cream. SERVES 6

FALL

king bolete

THE OYSTER TEST

WHEN MY SISTER got engaged, she made a point of flying to the West Coast with her newly betrothed so I could meet the lucky guy, my future brother-in-law. This was my younger sister, my only sister. As such, it occurred to me, based on the historical record, that I had a certain fraternal duty to uphold. Josh seemed nice enough. We stayed up late into the first evening listening to records. Musical tastes are important.

The next night my neighbor dropped by unexpectedly, as he has a habit of doing, and soon the three of us—me, Josh, and the neighbor—were involved in a beer-brewing episode that would carry us, again, deep into the night. As a stockpot of water, malt, and hops—known as the *wort*—boiled furiously, fogging windows throughout the house, we gave in to a great thirst. One of the arch-tenets of making beer is that you polish off the remnants of your previous batch while brewing. This both invites good luck and frees up empty bottles for the new batch.

Indeed, we seemed to be generating quite a few empties with which to house our new vintage when my neighbor disappeared back to his home and returned moments later with the biggest oysters I had ever seen. These were true monsters. Each one was longer than a small trout and weighed a couple of pounds at least. When quizzed on the origin of such impressive specimens, he offered up some vaguely contradictory mumblings about a load "off the back of a truck down south." Probably he'd been gambling at the Indian reservation again.

I'm with M.F.K. Fisher: my favorite way to eat oysters is naked. That is, raw on the half-shell with no adornments, not in the buff (although you'd be forgiven for dining on fresh oysters *au naturel*). Oyster eating is a sensual experience. It's a kiss of the sea—an activity fraught with sexual innuendo, and an extremely carnivorous one to boot. Consuming live animals is not generally part of the Western culinary canon. Of course, not all oysters are meant to be eaten raw. The gaggers, for instance. These I usually fry up for that Bourbon Street standard, the oyster po' boy, my second favorite way to eat them.

But I had special plans for these bigguns that didn't involve me.

When I get my own oysters, I usually take a jar with a screw-cap to hold whatever shucked oysters I don't eat directly off the beach. The limit is eighteen per day, and the shells must be returned whence they came to protect the native West Coast species, the diminutive Olympia oyster (*Ostrea lurida*)—named for the Washington State capital, where wild oyster harvesting was once a lucrative industry. Olympia seedlings, known as spat, prefer to anchor themselves on the shells of their elders, a process called setting. Baby oysters are free-floating plankton until they find a good place to set up shop, usually an estuarine habitat of salt water tempered by an influx of freshwater streams, and here they'll live out the rest of their days, filtering up to fifty gallons of tidewater a day. Since our native oyster was overharvested in the nineteenth and early twentieth centuries, before its lifecycle was fully understood, the young Olympias—in an ironic twist of imposed symbiotic fate—now use the shells of the nonnative and much more common Pacific oyster (*Crassostrea gigas*), introduced from Japan.

Pacific oysters—of which there are innumerable varieties, with names based on locale (Hog Island Sweetwaters, Westcott Bay

Petites, Deep Bay Kusshis)—are larger, with knobbier, fluted shells, and make up the bulk of the Northwest oyster trade. Three other species are commercially grown as well—the European flat (*Ostrea edulis*), sometimes referred to as a Belon, to the consternation of oyster growers in Brittany; the Kumamoto (*Crassostrea sikamea*), a Japanese import known for its sweet flavor; and the American Atlantic oyster (*Crassostrea virginica*). It wasn't so long ago that the most famous oysters in the country hailed from the East Coast—Wellfleets (Massachusetts), Apalachicolas (Florida), and Bluepoints (New York), to name a few. The honors have quietly moved westward more recently, with Washington's Puget Sound and Hood Canal oyster farmers wresting market share from the old standbys, and the growers of British Columbia's Strait of Georgia close behind. A well-stocked oyster bar in Seattle might offer a dozen or more local varieties today: Little Skookums, Totten Virginicas, Quilcenes, Penn Cove Selects, and so on.

We're fortunate that Washington State still has wild oyster beds open to the public, so satisfying a yearning for the plump, briny jewels of the sea doesn't necessarily mean a trip to the fish market or a pricey raw bar. My oyster gathering is mostly a side gig to whatever the primary outing is that day. Maybe I'm shrimping or fishing for salmon. But when the tide is right, I'll pull on the rubber boots and shuck some right where I'm standing and pop them into my mouth. All the better if I remember to bring a lemon and a good bottled beer. The rest of my limit goes into the jar. Sometimes I'll eat those raw as well when I get home, employing a shot glass and a spoonful of light mignonette for the purpose, but if they remain in the refrigerator for any length of time past a day, I'll cook them.

The po' boy is a celebrated Louisiana sandwich served on a French roll or baguette. Usual ingredients include shredded lettuce, thinly sliced tomatoes, and some sort of meat, often fried shrimp or oysters. The derivation of the name is disputed. One theory holds that it comes from a 1929 New Orleans streetcar strike, when a streetcar conductor–turned–restaurateur fed his former colleagues—called "poor boys"—free sandwiches from his shop. The po' boy is also known as an oyster loaf or Peace Maker: men carousing about town have traditionally brought home a Peace Maker to their wives at the end of a late night.

And for good reason. The po' boy is about the best sandwich you can imagine—even good enough to justify overlooking bad behavior. In my kitchen, the oysters get dipped in egg and then battered before being fried with a lot of butter. Next I prepare the rest of the sandwich: a soft French roll sliced open and slathered with mayonnaise and then topped with lettuce and tomatoes. Sometimes I add some hot peppers from Mama Lil. Lastly, I arrange the fried oysters on the bed of lettuce and draw a squiggly line of Frank's Red Hot Sauce from tip to tail. Cole slaw and potato chips finish the plate.

I save my outsized oysters for po' boys because, well, slamming down such a large, quivering pile of living flesh is more than even I can take. Which brings us back to Josh, my future brother-in-law, and the elephantine oysters before us. So far he'd been a really good sport, and I decided this would be the last hurdle: he was required to shoot the biggest, gnarliest oyster in the catch. It was as simple as that. I admitted right up front that this was a form of hazing that he would need to endure. What are brothers for, after all?

My neighbor agreed with the logic. We looked over the oysters, weighing them in our hands, tossing them back and forth to each other, admiring the barnacle condominiums perched on raised ridges of shell. Finally we settled on one. It was humongous. To open it we needed a hammer and chisel, and after several blows, when it finally parted, a cup of seawater—the liquor—drained out on the kitchen counter.

Josh looked it over. The meat alone was probably more substantial than a roasted squab. It glistened under fluorescent kitchen lights. We allowed him to cut the adductor muscles for easy sliding. He eyed a bottle of Tabasco on the counter and we acquiesced to that too. Then we all waited.

In the end, I suppose I wasn't disappointed that Josh ate the oyster—chewed it, even. But when he demanded a second one, I realized the tables had been turned. "C'mon," he said, holding up another bruiser as a briny toast, "join me. We'll be brothers soon." I'd sooner take a knife and make an incisive blood oath. Josh, I had to admit, had proven himself and more. Begging off the oversized bivalve, I retreated to the bubbling wort to lick my wounds, suddenly feeling small, more like a pesky little brother.

OYSTER PO' BOYS, OR PEACE MAKERS, FOR TWO

> ¼ cup flour
> ¼ cup cornmeal
> Salt to taste
> 1 dozen large oysters, shucked
> 1 egg, beaten
> Butter for frying
> 2 French rolls
> Mayonnaise
> Lettuce, shredded
> Tomato, thinly sliced
> Hot sauce

Combine flour and cornmeal on a plate and season liberally with salt. Dip oysters in egg, then dredge in the flour-cornmeal mixture. Fry battered oysters in butter. Meanwhile, prepare the sandwiches: Slice rolls and spread with mayo. Heap on lettuce, tomato, and whatever other condiments you prefer. When oysters are golden brown, remove them to paper towels to drain, then add them to sandwiches and decorate with hot sauce. Now hand one to long-suffering spouse. SERVES 2

THE GHOST OF ZANE GREY

WHEN I TOLD Warpo I was quitting my latest job and moving with Marty off the grid to caretake a rustic Oregon homestead in the woods near a famous fly-fishing river named the Rogue after a band of Indians who didn't give in easily to white conquest, he agreed it was about time. "I'll give you credit for outlasting everyone's predictions," he conceded. "You never were a company man."

I promised Warpo I'd send word when the steelhead arrived. Steelhead are fish right out of mythology—they're Homeric. Born in the coldest and swiftest streams of the West, they spend their first couple of years hidden in shady little pools until, one day, the urge to see the world comes over them. No more than a few inches long, they leave the safety of their rearing pools to drop down into currents that will bear them out to sea, dodging cormorants, seals, and pikeminnows along the way until they reach the great wide open of the Pacific, where they are transformed into the stuff of legend: large, powerful fish that break rods and leave human assailants shaken and muttering on the sidelines. A steelhead is the same species as a rainbow trout, but that's just a technicality. In reality it's the toughest, most ornery rainbow you've ever seen—with little resemblance to that piggy 'bow you find hanging around at the bottom of a reservoir growing fat on leeches like an overrated quarterback turned car salesman. It's a rainbow that's packed its bags and lit out for adventure.

Steelhead are anadromous, which means they spend part of their lives at sea and then return to their natal streams to spawn. The few that survive to produce the next generation are battle-tested by the Darwinian challenges of the hungry ocean. They grow long and streamlined and hard-bodied, and in the salt they lose the cute leopard spots and red lateral lines of their diminutive inriver relatives in exchange for grown-up silvery suits, dark on top and light below, the colors of oceanic predators relying on camouflage to ambush their prey. Maybe the gunmetal hue is what inspired the name—no one really knows for sure—but it sounds fitting just the same: these are hard-nosed fish, and to become attached to one is to learn the limitations of conventional trout tackle.

As interesting as the fish are those who pursue them. Steelheaders form a hermetic brotherhood, single-minded in the extreme, none more so than those who chase steelhead with a fly. A regular job would be an impossibility for many of them. Like itinerant mushroom pickers, they drive around the Northwest in beat-up fish-wagons doing a circuit: the first few months of the year are spent chasing rumors up and down hard-luck coastal towns like Forks, Washington, casting through frozen guides to sullen winter fish that may go in excess of fifteen pounds and leave reels smoked and in pieces on the gravel; then down to southern Oregon and Northern California for the summer-run openers on rivers like the North Umpqua; up to the Stillaguamish in Washington in August for the storied Deer Creek fish; north to British Columbia's renowned Skeena system for a good chunk of fall; then back down to the high desert plateau on broad-shouldered Columbia and Snake River tributaries like the Grande Ronde and Clearwater to close out the year. The steelheaders sleep in their vehicles and tie flies by headlamp; steaming cups of 7-11 coffee can't melt the icicles in their scraggly beards.

In the Pacific Northwest, steelhead are held in such high, iconic regard that, for a long time after moving here, I refused to fish for them—not out of reverence or anything, mostly out of fear. The fear of not measuring up, of being found out. Would the steelhead teach me a lesson I didn't want to learn? Would I discover something unpleasant about myself? Then I broke down and made a solo trip to the Olympic Peninsula one spring. I went alone so no one would see me. Somewhere along the road that leads to the Hoh rain forest I found a gap in the jungle and plunged my little car off the gravel and into a mud bog, emerging miraculously on a level bluff overlooking the river, with stout Douglas firs standing above me like glowering parents. I had a brand-new eight-weight flyrod that I had bought with a certain amount of embarrassment. "Go catch a steelhead," the clerk exhorted me after completing the sale, knowing I had just thrown my money away like all the other rubes who move to steelhead country.

The next day, though, to my astonishment, a spring buck of less than ten pounds in a river known for its twenty-pounders took a pink marabou confection, and it was all I could do to keep from accosting every drift boat with the news that I had just made my first acquaintance with the legendary steel.

Hooking a steelhead on the fly usually goes something like this: You cast. You cast again. And again. You cast all day and the next without so much as a bump. Then one morning, if you haven't yet traded in your rod for a set of golf clubs or stripped naked and run screaming down the road, the imaginary steelhead materializes out of nowhere to slam your fly before dashing downriver and disappearing once again into the depths, never to be seen again, giving you a heart attack in the process. Or, alternatively— and this is the real test—you detect just the slightest tug on the end of the line. The natural inclination is to jolt awake and strike as hard as you can so the fish—finally, the fish—doesn't get away, but in doing so, you yank the fly right out of its mouth.

On the other hand, if you have the presence of mind to stay calm, there is a moment of silence when the earth pauses in its rotation and the universe sighs. Don't flinch. The only one moving is the steelhead: after picking off your fly mid-drift—for reasons no one can adequately explain, because the great fish is not feeding in any true sense of the word—it's turning and heading back to its former resting spot, the fly still clamped in its jaw. If you can bear to watch the extra slack line in your hand slip out through the rod guides without coming unglued, you have a chance. Lift the rod tip gently. The line tightens, and the hook-point catches and sticks in the corner of the steelhead's mouth. You have another nanosecond of quiet. You might even pause to consider how beautiful the steelhead's home is. A light mist hovers over the river, and the distant mountains are dusted with snow.

Then all hell breaks loose.

The fish comes cartwheeling out of the water as if it could climb each airborne splash like a staircase to steelhead asylum. It crashes back beneath the glittering surface and takes off on a burning run downstream. Provided your reel is up to the task and hasn't busted a nut or woven a bird's nest of line, you check the fish just before it reaches the rapids, deep into your backing. The next minute is spent reeling furiously as you run down the bank like a clown in your wading boots, galumphing and shouting. You turn the fish upstream and it takes another screaming run, this time leaping a few feet into the air at the end. More runs and tailwalking until you have it in the shallows. Now is the time to really lay on the cork. The fish is tired and you need to act quickly. In a few inches of water you're able to tail it and remove the fly. It's a magnificent fish, nickel-bright. You want to kiss it.

Time out! Upon closer scrutiny, you notice that the small fin behind the dorsal is missing. This phantom limb is known as the adipose fin, and it's mostly vestigial. The lack of an adipose can mean only one thing: it was deliberately clipped by a human being to mark it as such. The steelhead you want to smooch is actually a hatchery-bred fish. Now you have to make a decision. Do you whack it?

Among a certain segment of steelhead addicts, the idea of killing even a hatchery fish is heresy—and it is here that I part ways with the wild-eyed believers. Hatchery steelhead fillets taste delicious in any setting, but the taste of one roasted over a bed of coals in the outback, miles away from anywhere, is almost beyond description. Such a meal makes the notion of "camp food" seem quaint and vaguely Stone Age. The flesh of steelhead is a lighter pink than salmon, and more delicate. It flakes nicely and crisps on the edges with a caramelized sweetness when exposed directly to the flame. The taste is somewhere between that of a trout and a salmon. Native Americans revered steelhead as food, and other mammals are known to nurse a sweet tooth for the sea-run trout as well. Sea lions have learned to hang around fish ladders below dams, where they pick off endangered native steelhead while ignoring more common races of salmon, much to the alarm of sportsmen, environmentalists, and fisheries biologists.

Anyhow, I can appreciate the fanatic's reasons for returning a hatchery fish to the river. I've done it myself. It's a generous gesture. Perhaps some other die-hard will now have a shot at the same steelhead another day. Lord knows it's hard enough to hook these critters to begin with, so the more fish in the river, the better your chances. On the other hand, hatchery fish pose problems for their already beleaguered wild cousins. Some of them forgo the hatchery terminus and try to go native, diluting the gene pool in the process. In this sense, eating a hatchery fish is doing a good turn for the wild ones still in the river.

Like salmon, hatchery steelhead are propagated through test-tube insemination and raised in concrete "runs." When they reach the right size, usually several inches, the young fish are released back into the rivers to smolt (that is, go out to sea). After anywhere from one to three years at sea, the adults return to the hatchery of their birth, where their eggs and milt are extracted to artificially spawn the next generation.

Steelheaders have a lot of colorful names for hatchery fish:

they call them brats, clones, rubber fish, zombies, and so on. You get the idea. They're not held in quite the same esteem as wild steelhead. These engineered fish tend to be uniform in size and shape, and generally smaller. The males, or bucks, often lack the physical features that wild female fish find attractive in mates, such as broad shoulders and kyped jaws. And most anglers would say they lack the fight of a wild fish, although this point is debatable; after all, a returning hatchery fish has survived the rigors of the seas, even if it began life with a silver spoonful of fish pellets. In any event, many steelheaders and supporters of wild fish would like to see the hatcheries done away with once and for all.

Ironically, this sad situation is the result of an effort that began more than a century ago and had such success with rainbow trout that those nonmigratory fish are now established all over the world. The national fish hatchery scheme was launched by President Ulysses S. Grant in 1871, when he signed the U.S. Fish Commission into existence. Soon after, the commission dispatched renowned aquaculturist Livingston Stone to California to establish the first U.S. hatchery. Stone picked the McCloud River, a headwater tributary of the Sacramento River near Mount Shasta, a "region which is just as it was before the white man found it, and with a race of aborigines whose simple habits have not been corrupted by the aggressive influence of communication with the whites." His initial efforts with salmon eggs met with mixed results, but after relocating to another stretch of the McCloud, Stone hit pay dirt with rainbow trout. In the coming years rainbows would be exported all over the United States and to every continent. Though it is not known to what degree the rainbow trout of the McCloud had anadromy in their genes, virtually every population of native rainbows that isn't landlocked will produce steelhead, so one can only assume that all those punter rainbows stocked across the globe have a little bit of steelie in them.

After succeeding with trout propagation, the feds learned how to breed Pacific salmon, and in time the hatcheries were used as a political tool to sidestep the negative effects of resource exploitation and development. Each new dam or other disturbance was sold to the public with a mitigating hatchery and assurances that fish runs would continue, thanks to the miracle of modern science. As we know now, it didn't quite work out that way. Nature turned out to be a better provider than fisheries biologists, but by the time this seemingly obvious truism was recognized, it was too late for many rivers and their wild fish.

The Columbia River system, once the greatest salmon and steelhead factory of them all, was transformed into a series of slackwater impoundments, making Lewiston, Idaho, a deepwater port and Grand Coulee Dam the end of the line, with thousands of miles of streams beyond it purged of seagoing fish. The consequences are only now coming into focus, yielding some startling insights, such as the recent finding that salmon, whose decomposing bodies become food for birds, bears, and other critters, account for one of the main nitrogen-fixing agents in inland forests. The big old-growth trees of the West, some of them older than Columbus, literally stand on the backs of dead salmon.

Today the worst-offending hatcheries are being mothballed, and biologists are trying to ensure that the remaining hatchery fish don't dilute wild strains any more than they already have. It's a typical story of hubris. As for steelhead fishermen in the Northwest, the decline of the fish is such that there are few rivers left where one can kill a wild steelhead, and those who elect to do so are often shunned like lepers. For many, even taking home a hatchery fish just doesn't feel right.

Zane Grey needn't have pondered such byzantine ethical dilemmas. In his day, all the fish were wild. And there were enough of them that an angler could go out and catch a bunch on a good day and keep a nice one for dinner. No doubt Grey enjoyed numerous steelhead meals at his retreat on Winkle Bar. Best known today to floaters who navigate southwestern Oregon's Rogue River through thirty-four miles of rapids in the federally designated Wild and Scenic lower river canyon, Winkle Bar is one of those places where steelhead like to hang out. Just past the fifteen-mile mark downstream of Grave Creek is the bar, a long gravel reach and meadow. Keeping watch from above is an old rough-hewn cabin built by the sportsman-novelist who gave us such sentimental and overwrought Wild West tales as *Riders of the Purple Sage* as well as volumes of high-flown adventure writing.

Grey first heard about sea-run rainbow trout while in the Florida Keys, from a displaced salmon fisherman who talked about a type of fish that "smashed his tackle." He visited the Rogue Valley a few times in the early 1920s and caught his first Rogue River steelhead near Grants Pass in 1922, a moment that occasioned this ripe soliloquy: "If moments could be wholly all-satisfying with thrills and starts, and dreads and hopes, and vague, deep, full sense of the wild beauty of the environment, and the vain boyish joy in showing my comrades my luck and my skill—if any moments of life could utterly satisfy, I experienced them then."

But mostly his initial efforts struck him as unworthy. For one thing, he deemed his tackle all wrong, bemoaning a reel with far from adequate backing to hold the hard-running fish and useless flies. Two years later, determined to learn to catch steelhead on a fly, he camped on the Rogue for a few fall weeks with his brother R.C. and several other invited guests, including a man known as the Captain, who had fished for Atlantic salmon with a fly. In his story about the trip, "Rocky Riffle," he wonders whether the Rogue is the perfect fishing destination. His brother suggests it would be even better if they could find a riffle "unfrequented by strings of city anglers and crowds of native fishermen," to which the author responds by imagining a float trip down the remote lower river, adding as a tantalizing hook: "So far as I know it has never been fished." The scene is set for "Down River," Grey's next account of the Rogue, a 1925 expedition through the wild canyon known to only a handful of prospectors and settlers. With seven wooden boats and a party of ten men, including his son,

he floated the lower Rogue from below Galice to its mouth at
Gold Beach, running the river's famous rapids and leaving at least
one boat wrecked on the rocks.

During that trip he camped at a bonny spot known as
Winkle Bar and vowed to "get possession" of it from the miner
who owned the claim. He did, and the following year, in the late
summer of 1926, the well-heeled writer hired muleskinners to
pack him overland into the canyon. The lead packer brought no
fewer than sixteen mules, eight saddle horses, and a couple of
his own sons to hump the author's tackle and that of several relatives and associates. The trip was twenty miles one-way from the
now defunct West Fork railroad station on Cow Creek, through
a dark wilderness of vaulting firs. They camped on Winkle Bar,
where Grey would build the spare one-room cabin that still
stands on a green bluff overlooking the river.

I learned about Zane Grey's exploits on the Rogue from a
1928 first edition of his *Tales of Freshwater Fishing*. The final 175
pages—a half-dozen stories in all—concern the author's growing love affair with the Rogue River. I devoured the stories for
their glimpses into the past of a river canyon I now called home,
as well as for any nuggets of wisdom I could extract about how
to fish for steelhead. The writing is breezy and descriptive. By
today's standards the style would be roundly dismissed for its
endless cowboy vistas and exclamation points, but purple prose
aside, Zane Grey knew a good fishing hole when he saw one,
and when you get past the rosy dawns and dark ramparts and
singing reels, there are some timeless bits of angling wisdom. "I
often wonder if I do not care too much about fish and fishing,"
he writes, echoing a sentiment known to any angler who worries
about his addiction. "Such a mental attitude does not enhance
skill, and it certainly seems to be a lodestone for ill luck."

Luck, or the lack of it, is a theme that runs through all the
stories. Grey is frequently bested by his companions, and when
his moment arrives he is usually lost in reverie, too busy admiring a sunset or observing the curious dips of a water ouzel to set

the hook properly. Though he has the good form to make fun of his slipups, it's clear that a competitive atmosphere exists in camp. Each fish is weighed and tallied, and the one that got away is hardly a footnote.

Today's steelheader can only shake his head at the fishing described in these pages. These were the formative years of steelhead angling in America, with only a select band of mystics trying to catch them on a fly. Even without the benefit of modern tackle and a century's worth of fine-tuned technique, Grey and his friends still managed to raise fish after fish—and on dry flies to boot. At night, in my bed, with nothing but darkness outside my window, I tried to imagine the Rogue as the author had experienced it, before the surrounding hills were denuded and the river impounded and dynamited along its race to the sea.

For his part, Grey was well traveled enough to know that he was witness to a passing age. In his writings he denounced the advance of the automobile and referred to the wild places of the West mournfully, in capitals, as Vanishing America. While he was ahead of his time in this respect, his editors were not, and they frequently chopped down his brief inveighments against the wholesale destruction of the once-vast wilderness. One passage that survives, from "Rocky Riffle," laments the cutting of the old-growth forests and the effects on wildlife, though Grey admits that little is to be done without the "interest of the great public in preserving anything."

As promised, I summoned Warpo in early October. After collecting him at the optimistically named Medford International Airport (where he was leaning casually against a post with his tackle bag tucked under his arm the way James Dean might have done it—if he were a fisherman—and singing the refrain to "A Shenandoah Lullaby"), I used the drive home to counsel my old friend, a steelhead novice, on what lay ahead. I had been fishing nearly every evening since Labor Day. My efforts had been rewarded mostly with "half-pounders," those hotheaded juvenile

steelhead that take over the lower Rogue like gang members in
a turf war. Here and there, though, I had managed to sneak a
fly past this hair-trigger gauntlet to entice the more circumspect
elders, adult fish on spawning runs that weighed anywhere from
three to ten pounds. These sea-runs put my soft six-weight rod
to the test, with more than one knitting my flimsy trout reel into
a fright wig of overspin.

I explained all this to Warpo. I explained how patience and
fortitude would see us through, how becoming one with the
wilderness was the secret to success. He listened in uncharacteristic silence as we left the houses, farms, and pavement behind.
Soon there was only darkness beyond the headlights. The rhyth-
mic jouncing over dirt road was comforting, and it put me in an
expansive mood. We still had a long drive ahead. There was no
hurry. The steelhead would be holding in their usual lies behind
rocks and camouflaged in gravel runs. They would be waiting
for us.

To know Warpo and his lineage was to be reminded of the
days of crossing Drosophila fruit flies in biology class. Such a
specimen seemed impossible without a coerced hybridization
under glass. And yet here he was, so obviously a product of his
parents that you wondered how these two people stayed together
long enough to pass on their wildly differing strands of DNA.

From his mother, a generous, dreamy, academic-minded sort
who dabbled in Shakespeare and mysticism, Warpo inherited
a bent for abstraction and flights of fancy. The first time I met
his mother, she inquired about my sun sign and enumerated—
accurately—a number of my own character traits. Next she
told me about the time she had assumed the consciousness of a
houseplant. Warpo's father, a big-time architect and a bigger-time
proponent of tough love, lived in Boston in a stately Beacon Hill
townhouse. Upon our first introduction, he insisted that I was
antisocial and lectured the two of us in his gruff manner about
our weak moral fiber. Warpo acquired from him his height, his
pathological stubbornness, a spatial awareness that often seemed

at odds with his imagination, and a do-it-yourself approach to virtually any task, large or small.

Warpo's real name is Joseph, but unlike a lot of college friends who reverted to their less colorful given names once they took jobs at banks and law firms and insurance companies, Joe was still Warpo to me, and I made a point of keeping the name alive, much to his wife's chagrin. The name's aura of straddling multiple dimensions and courting an unintended yet perfectly natural eccentricity had suited Warpo in his younger days (with his paisley shirts, his broken front tooth, and the jug of cheap wine he always carried with him), and though he blended in with the crowd later on, I knew better.

Warpo was tall and sinewy, with long, loose-jointed limbs and a tremendous Roman nose that gave his otherwise thin face a sense of solemnity. He had a habit of knocking things over or tripping on alien objects. Sometimes he wore a beard, sometimes not; sometimes his hair was a corolla of unmanageable curls, sometimes it was shorn to the nubbin. Now he lived in Virginia, where he was a fine woodworker by trade, building furniture and cabinetry and the like. When I was best man at his wedding, he built me a correspondence box from reclaimed wormwood and antique hobnails, and though it hasn't seen a lot of action in this age of email, the box still contains all my topo maps, which somehow seems fitting. Even with this handsome reminder on my desk, though, it was still hard to picture Warpo nestled in his basement shop, contained and reasonable, instructing his extremities to make the fine calibrations necessary for his trade; instead, I saw him swinging a giant framing hammer and kicking out walls.

Back at the house we sat outside on the deck and examined Warpo's flies. It was quiet. Marty was in town for a poetry reading. The air was warm for an October night, and giant orange caddis buzzed the kerosene lamp. Warpo explained that he had found some great deals online. He plucked one fly after another out of his box, each one gaudier than the last, saying, "This is the one….No, *this* is the one. Look at this mother, this is hooking me some steel." He held up to the lamplight an enormous concoction in green and white, more appropriate for bluefin tuna in the South Pacific, followed by an even more preposterous study in pink, an exploding fuchsia hairball, its hook hidden somewhere beneath a mountain of fluff.

"Hmm, Warpo…is that the famous Park Avenue muff pattern? Or is it an LPGA golf club cover?"

Warpo looked at me with sudden confusion. "What? You're saying these aren't good steelhead flies?" Then he uncorked his horselaugh and filled the canyon with uncontrolled mirth.

"Go ahead," I said. "There's no one around for miles. No driveways, no lights, no nothing."

The next morning was perfect steelhead weather—cool, damp, the tops of the trees hidden in a fast-moving fog that coiled and uncoiled like a spectral constrictor snake. Unlike every other angler in the canyon, we would be on foot. I suppose I could have rented a drift boat, but the idea of walking beneath a ceiling of dark primeval forest, rod in hand, appealed to me. We planned to take our time. There were mushrooms to hunt, steelhead to catch, unfrequented corners of the canyon to explore.

We packed light. On my previous trips into the canyon I had always managed to catch a nice steelhead. I told Warpo not to worry about food. I purposefully packed less of the nasty, freeze-dried camper's food than we would need, remarking gravely that it was incumbent on us to catch or otherwise forage a good deal of our nourishment. "If we really get into trouble," I said, "we can always eat a mess of half-pounders." He scoffed openly at this idea—me telling him that we would need to switch to survival mode. Warpo grew up largely on a farm in Vermont. He was catching pan fish as soon as he could walk and gigging frogs for a change of scenery. His father sent him away to outdoor leadership schools virtually every summer of his teens to be toughened and learn the art of wilderness travel. He had worked on a fishing boat in Alaska and spent a winter snowbound in a tent in the Sangre de Cristo Mountains of New Mexico. "Don't you worry about me, Hoss," he said. "What I'd like to see is whether you have the nuts to kill one of those beautiful little fish."

Those beautiful little fish, called "half-pounders" by the locals, are immature steelhead that run up the Rogue for reasons scientists have yet to fully understand. Too young to spawn, they enter fresh water in the late summer and loiter all winter, eating just enough to stay alive, then drop back down to the salt to finish maturing before their actual spawning run the next fall. It's a puzzling phenomenon that occurs in only a handful of watersheds along the Oregon-California border. Fly-fishermen in particular admire the half-pounders, which generally tape out between twelve and sixteen inches and lustily take a fly, providing good sport when the big fish aren't ready to play.

In the Rogue the half-pounders were common through the canyon we planned to hike, whereas adult steelhead usually blasted through this turbulent stretch of water to reach the broader gravelly runs upriver. But Winkle Bar was one spot where I had almost always hooked a big steelhead in the canyon, and it was here that I hoped we would catch an adult hatchery fish that could make a feast for a couple of trail-weary backpackers. I had plans in store. "Forget about the little guys," I said. "We're going to do the wild steelhead of the Rogue a favor and eat one of those hatchery imposters." Warpo, who almost surely had a tapeworm, would experience a backwoods feast that would overwhelm even his notorious appetite. And just in case we caught a steelhead big enough to provide both dinner and lunch the next day, I had a small jar of unopened mayonnaise and several hard rolls in my pack. Steelhead-salad sandwiches were about the best lunch a backpacker could dream of on the trail.

With high hopes, we started out. The pack felt heavy and good on my back. After negotiating several miles of exposed trail high above the river, we dropped down to find a hectic stretch of pocket water, good half-pounder habitat. Warpo had never

fly-fished with a sinking tip line before, so as a demonstration
I stripped some line off my rod and chucked the fly out in the
middle, a Rogue River Red Ant. I had bought the materials for
this long-standing local fly from an ancient Navy veteran who
ran the Silver Sedge Fly Shoppe in town. The hooks seemed
large for fish of this size, I had said to him; should I drop down a
size? "Those half-pounders may not be big," he told me in a rasp
that spoke of multiple ports of call, "but they don't know it."

The fly hadn't been in the water more than a second when
a fourteen-inch fish grabbed it, dashed out of sight, then
reemerged to perform three great aerial flips in a row before
coming to hand. So much for a casting demonstration. I held up
the young steelhead for Warpo to see. It gleamed silver, with just
the faintest nod to the spots and red lateral line of its resident,
untraveled kin. Unlike a lake-bound rainbow or one of those
overfed tailwater footballs, this one was lean and hard, without
the slightest hint of indulgence. "That was supposed to be your
fish," I apologized, releasing it back into the riffle.

"I think I'll go find my own piece of water."

Just then, a loud buzzing noise interrupted the muffled canyon silence. A prop plane cut through the fogbank and flew low
overhead, going upriver. Warpo instinctively dropped down,
looking for cover, and not because he's a tall man used to ducking. Let me just state for the record that Warpo is one of the
kindest, most thoughtful people I know. That doesn't change the
fact that in his younger days he courted a sort of fly-by-night
spontaneity—some might call it recklessness—that was, at times,
at odds with the oath of law enforcement officers.

Seeing Warpo wince now at the overflight took me back
many years to a brief period when we had recently become liber-
ated from our educational duties and immediately drove west to
San Francisco to seek our fortunes. Each morning we careened
down the hill from our apartment in the Haight, Warpo captain-
ing his unregistered and uninsured '65 Volkswagen microbus in
neutral, I suppose to save on fuel, running every red light until

we hit the Mission District flats, where he would finally punch the gas and we'd sputter over to the job site on Folsom. For several months we worked on the same Victorian, burning off its old coat and restoring the intricate façade to its former glory with no fewer than a dozen different pastel colors.

By the end of the job—after a third painter had set the house on fire with a propane torch and someone had spilled a bucket of primer on the owner's Mercedes and we had witnessed a knife fight in the street over a parking spot—after it was all done and over, the house looked stunning. Warpo moved to an apartment near the Tenderloin and not long after that got into a scuffle over an unregistered motorcycle. Police in a cruiser chased him through Chinatown until he took a wrong turn into a dead end littered with chicken bones. "They beat me," he said with astonishment and genuine hurt feelings, his leather jacket and chaps torn from a high-speed skid in the alleyway. "They beat me like a common criminal." The motorcycle was gone, the money from the painting job nearly spent. That night was the last I saw of him for some time. Just after midnight we finished packing up his microbus and sent him and his cat out of state under the cover of darkness before he could get into serious trouble.

Fast-forward a decade and Warpo is whispering in my ear at a taco bar in New York City. "See that girl? I'm going to marry her." A year later he did, and now he was a father, a respected craftsman, and a man who had a hankering for steelhead.

Unbeknownst to Warpo, a copy of Zane Grey's Rogue River writings accompanied us in my pack. I saw my first chance at oratory near Kelsey Creek. Warpo had found himself a nice rocky seat from which to cast, where the canyon narrowed and a series of vertical cliffs impeded passage along the banks. The river ran fast through its slot before dumping into a deep, churning hole. Behind his throne, a crowd of leafy trees clamored for a sight of the Rogue.

It was a tough cast, with branches behind him and white

water below. But right out in front, where the river ran honest, several submerged boulders were sure to shelter the largest steelhead in the run. It was an impossibly minuscule sweet spot, but a sweet spot nonetheless. If he managed a hookup, Warpo would need to act fast to turn the fish before it could head downstream into the churn. The situation reminded me of a passage out of "Rocky Riffle":

My line straightened out with fly sunk. Then came a vicious tug. Quick as a flash I struck and hooked what felt like a log. Down river he raced and my reel sang. He did not leap. With wagging rod held high—no easy task—I began to wade out and down. But I could not make fast enough time. I wallowed, plunged. Then I forgot to hold the loose click on my reel. It slipped off, releasing the drag, and the spool whizzed. I felt a hard jerk—then a slack line.

I was about to bring the book over for our entertainment when Warpo hollered. From my position on the rocks downriver I could just make out his yell of "Got 'em!" over the roar of rapids. Then he stood up on his throne and I could see the wagging of his bent-over rod. Line tore through the guides. Though I couldn't actually hear the reel singing, I could see the angle of the line slicing downstream toward the ocean. An eyeblink later his fish reached the white water and Warpo was visibly fumbling with a reel burning up in his hand. Seconds before he lost all his line and backing, he clamped down on the rim with one hand and pointed his rod at his quarry with the other. Again, because of my position and the rumble of the river, I could not hear anything. Still, the hollow popping sound of a fish breaking its tether to the land was manifested in the sight of the line ballooning gracefully up in the air and coming to rest in the tree branches behind. The howl of disbelief and protest that came next I did hear, despite the thousands of cubic feet per second rushing past.

We gathered up our packs and got back on the trail. Warpo didn't say anything for a while. It was tough to let go of such fish. They pulled at your sense of yourself as an angler: What could I have done differently? Was I slow to react? Did I set up correctly? Am I a pathetic loser? In the end there was no accounting for it.

After detouring around numerous steep ravines, each one containing a small creek speeding toward its appointment with the Rogue, we found a side trail leading down out of the forest and across a great flat meadow—Winkle Bar. The cabin was a simple one-room affair constructed from timbers cut by hand on-site. A heavy rope of the sort you might find in a theater or museum barred entry through the front door, so we settled on a dark glimpse through the window. The bed was made. A round woven rug decorated the worn wooden floor. Over to the side stood a small desk with the requisite manual typewriter atop it, probably long since frozen up. This was where Grey retreated from the strenuous life of the world's best-selling author, where he recuperated from months at sea in the tropics and North Atlantic trying to set big-game fishing records, where he left behind his mistresses and other cares. "Call it what you will," said Warpo, "but he didn't build this himself. He hired someone."

"Someone like you," I reminded my friend, "who he paid well, no doubt. Besides, give him credit for the location."

There was no denying the appeal of Winkle Bar, with its broad meadows and its nearby groves of impressive trees, with its picture-perfect riffles and runs. Grey writes of his first view of the bar, from a high point overlooking the canyon: "Directly below, the river dark and still between lofty cliffs that faced out of the dense forest. Ducks with white barred wings floated on the light mirroring water, and salmon breaking on the surface spread ever-widening circles. Across the river a magnificent fir forest rose out of a five-sloped canyon, rising bearded and mossy and black, to the far, ragged summits."

Yes, he picked one of the better locations for a cabin. More important, as far as we were concerned—and probably for Grey too—the bar could boast one of the prime gravel runs in the canyon. Adult steelhead feel comfortable and secure holding in such water. They blend in with the cobbles and don't have to worry about predators. Much of the canyon is scoured bedrock— narrow coindrops, fast chutes, deep rifts—good half-pounder holding water but not right for the big fish migrating upstream to spawn. The adults need to rest near the bottom of slower, walking-pace stretches with stones and gravel. Like a greenbelt that attracts birds migrating over a city, this quarter mile of river served as a rest stop for big fish. It was a classic Northwest steelhead run—calendar material, really—with a boisterous riffle at the top that surrendered to a long seam, perhaps two hundred yards, before emptying into an elbow pool of disturbed roiling water and another long riffle-run.

Looking upstream was an exercise in conjuring a lost wilderness, Grey's Vanishing America. Great tumbling ridges of primeval forest slanted down to the river, each one a lighter blue than the last as they receded into the hazy, sunspotted distance. Not until the nearest bend did the river itself suddenly slice into view, a thin ribbon of gray that banked again and widened out, a hundred yards across and shallow, before narrowing back into its corset. The trees running down the canyon's embankments stuck out at odd angles, some of them in the unhurried process of losing their grip on the land and hanging precariously over the river, ready to be swept away should they continue their slow-motion pitch toward the water. The entire stretch whispered steelhead, and in the morning it made a lovely sight with the mist rising off the back eddies.

We pitched our tent in the sand and rigged up. "Now, Hoss," Warpo started in, "do I go with the Muddler or one of these bead-headed Woolly Buggers?" I suggested a much smaller, drabber pattern. Warpo was outraged. "That little thing? What self-respecting sea-run trout of double-digit proportions is going to give a rat's ass about a scraggly pipsqueak of a fly like that?"

"It's a learning curve. Zane Grey went through the same process." I reached into the tent for the book. "Right here, he talks about his revelation: light lines and smaller flies." Warpo listened as I read the passage aloud.

"That was what, more than eighty years ago?" He started to walk down to the river. I tossed the book back on my sleeping bag.

"So."

"So, no matter how much people of our ilk may object, it's a new world now. Marketing, advertising, getting your product noticed. I'm going with the big and flashy."

"Listen to yourself. I can't believe what I'm hearing. Is this Contrarian Warpo talking, or some pod-person that's invaded his hollowed-out husk of a body?" I knew I was inviting a long disquisition on the consumer response patterns of sea-run rainbows, or on the very nature of desire itself—one that might tie together strands of ecology, the Victoria's Secret catalog, and of course the wood-fiber business—but instead Warpo was silent, his head bowed. There at our feet, like a sinister version of pickup sticks, lay dozens of clean white skeletons. The remains of young steelhead.

"It's a massacre."

Though my friend was taken aback, I'd seen it all before. Large parties of fishermen floated the Rogue at this time of year, hiring several guides and a string of drift boats. They fished for chinook salmon and steelhead. Half-pounders, aggressive and uneducated, ended up in the coolers in stacks. I'd see the groups hauled out on the banks for lunch, the guides preparing a half-pounder feast for their clients over little gas grills. The fishermen showed little restraint. They just couldn't resist such easy pickings. Each fish got tossed into the creel. Internet message boards were apoplectic over the practice. One steelhead fisherman vented his frustration by shouting in all caps, "LITTLE STEELIES GROW UP TO BE BIG STEELIES. STOP THE SLAUGHTER!!!"

But it was legal to kill fin-clipped hatchery fish. And while it was true that the hatchery fish were in the river for the sole purpose of harvest, it was also true that for every half-pounder in the frying pan, there was one less fully grown steelhead a year or two later to rip the line off your reel and send your heart into palpitations.

We trudged in silence upstream to the head of the riffle. Warpo stepped in above me and tossed his fly out into the whirl-pool of white water. There was no sense in trying to mend line; a swirling current sucked his fly under and out of view in a flash. Another cast and he let out a whoop. First strike. He cast again and was tight to a half-pounder of fifteen or more inches.

"I guess they left us a few." He released the fish back into the turbulence. Without a word spoken, we had agreed that we would not make a dinner of the half-pounders. We worked down through the run. I switched to a more natural fly, a Hare's Ear nymph with a few strands of tinsel flash for a wing, and started picking up half-pounders at the end of the swing. Somewhere out there, finning near the bottom by itself, was a large adult steelhead. Warpo tied on a Green-butt Skunk and immediately felt the rod jerked out of his hand. "Big fish," he started to say, and then the line went slack. He stood there, mouth agape, unable to move. I knew the feeling.

Soon evening was upon us and neither one of us had hooked into a legitimate steelhead, not for more than a second or two at least. Autumn darkness came quickly to the canyon bottom. My idea of a gourmet steelhead dinner in Zane Grey country was for naught. We built a fire and ate canned stew along with rationed pulls off a flask of Beam, and though we didn't have enough liquor to get seriously maudlin, I was nevertheless feeling the weight of all those dead half-pounders, of the streams I had fished long ago that were now lined with houses, of the clear-cut forest over the next ridge. Trips into the wilderness always made me realize just how tenuous this life really was. Of course you expect all your friends to live forever when you're young. Warpo in particular seemed immune to the reaper. He had wrecked multiple cars and put himself in harm's way more times than I could count. Did I say that out loud?

Warpo snorted through his distinguished nose. "Whatever doesn't kill us makes us stronger," he said, unafraid even to traffic in cliché.

Later, in the middle of the night, I shot out of my sleeping bag with a start and looked outside the tent flap. In the distance the glowing eyes of deer burned in the blackness. Closer in, I saw Warpo. He was bent over as if carrying a heavy burden, walking around outside the tent, kicking sand and muttering to himself. I crawled out and shone my headlamp in his eyes. Warpo crinkled up his face and rubbed his temples. I could see his expression begin to shift out of unconsciousness.

"There's a good reason why I'm walking naked through the wilderness, if I could just remember it. Is Zane Grey still in there?"

"You're in your long johns."

Warpo looked down. "Oh, good. Anyway, I'm not sharing a tent with that guy."

"He's dead and gone."

"He sleeps with a steelhead under his pillow."

"Nothing to worry about. Back in you go." Warpo got back in his sleeping bag and was immediately asleep. I stared outside the flap, watching pairs of eyes move around in the night until they faded into nothingness.

The sky was clear the next morning, with a pale yellow streak to the east riding shotgun in advance of the sun. There was a chill on the air that would be erased by noon. A grainy vapor hovered over the river's surface like a cloud of translucent midges with only minutes to live. We pulled on the waders again and started at the top of the run. More than once Warpo felt a violent tug on his line, one of which made off with his fly, but the big steelhead evaded us. Perhaps it was only just. Hooking and landing a steelhead on a freshman trip is like losing your virginity on a first date. By all rights it shouldn't happen, and if it does, your fishing career, guided so much by planning and anticipation and the bittersweet memory of the near miss, is permanently wrecked. No, there would be no roll in the hay with a great fish this time out.

As I made peace with this fact I found myself pulling more and more line off the reel and shooting tremendous casts out across the riffles. Tremendous for me, in any case. A sliver of sun peeked above the eastern rim of the canyon. The steelhead hour was nearly over. Soon the mist would be gone and light would inch across the river, transforming its dark broken surface into millions of uncut diamonds reflecting the brilliance of this happily forsaken canyon. I felt the seconds ticking off in the metronome of my casting arm. The line made a pleasant pulse of wind as it whipped back and forth above my head and then unfurled out over the water.

Upstream in the fast water Warpo was working his own line with similar resolve. Fishing was nearly over and yet the day was just beginning. Odd notions enter the mind under such purgatorial conditions. Already I was laying plans for the next trip. It occurred to me that I had known Warpo for nearly twenty years. One day, hopefully, we would take our children down a river like this together, fishing the runs, camping on the bars, telling stories by firelight. A new run of steelhead would be in, following their age-old yearning upstream. Somewhere beneath those riffles they would nose in the current. The river flowing on.

On the way out we came upon the Zane Grey cabin again. I told Warpo about how the author of a mythical West eventually abandoned his once-cherished Rogue Canyon for other less trammeled haunts, including the remote North Umpqua, a place of reportedly unimaginable beauty and natural wealth—a place that would fall, in turn, to the lumberers and developers.

Past the empty cabin we ran into a middle-aged woman with uncombed hair and a slightly wild look in her eyes, as if she had been wandering these hills for a while in search of something that continued to elude her. She was wearing a sweatsuit with little Christmas designs on it, green wreaths and red bulbs and that sort of thing. This strange apparition, it turned out, was the wife of the Zane Grey cabin caretaker, and she was in fact looking for something, a black cat. She had come down nearly two miles of roughed-out trail from her home 1,500 feet above us, where she had raised a whole family off the grid, beyond the pull of society.

No, we said, we hadn't seen her pet. With that, she was moving off in the other direction toward an unkempt meadow where a hungry cat might wait for a bird or mouse to make a fatal mistake. I called after her, wanting to know what her husband the caretaker did and trying to make neighborly conversation, but her mind was on the cat. "Who owns all this?" I finally shouted, and she stopped and turned around. "That's a good question." She told us the property was an inholding owned by a wealthy family from California who never used it. It might go up for sale, she said. Apparently a local historical society was trying to persuade the state to purchase the property—"that would be the best solution for all of us," she added—but the state was crying poverty. I looked around, taking in the shake cabin and the long airstrip of plush grass beyond it, the riverside willows and forested hills in the distance. It was not hard to imagine a single white real estate sign tacked up to a metal stake in front of the cabin where Zane Grey had tried to relax. Warpo saw it too. "It's all for sale," he murmured as the lady looking for her cat disappeared out of sight.

"The steelhead don't know that," I reminded him. "When the next ice age wipes out all of this, they'll retreat south to streams coming off the Sierra Madres."

Warpo rolled this possibility around in his head. "Fishing for steelhead in Mexico...I like that idea."

BARBECUED HATCHERY STEELHEAD

As a conservationist and member of the Wild Steelhead Coalition, I can't condone the killing of a wild steelhead in its native range, especially a trophy fish. Those twenty-pounders are needed for the gene pool if anglers want to catch and release big steelhead in the future. That said, for better or worse, hatchery steelhead have been planted in rivers throughout the Northwest and elsewhere so that an angler can eat his catch—and what a catch it is. If you're lucky and skilled enough to take home a hatchery steelhead, do it the honor of a barbecue burial. Unlike Pacific salmon, the taste of steelhead is subtle enough that spicy rubs and heavy sauces can overshadow the delicate flavor. I prefer a simple salt-and-pepper seasoning and olive oil. The key is getting a crisp edge on the fish without overcooking it.

If you haven't eaten steelhead before, imagine fresh sautéed rainbow trout with a hint of the sea to it, an essence of shrimp or crab that expands the flavor without losing that fine, nutty troutness. It's a noble taste that should be enjoyed with good friends.

But remember: more often than not, the steelhead fisherman will return home with only the taste of the river and the trees and the polished stones on his lips. For the true steelhead fisherman, this should be—will have to be—enough.

CONFESSIONS OF AN AMANITA EATER

THE FALL RAINS came early. For a week in September, storm clouds clogged up the canyon and hinted at colder, wetter days to come, with the possibility of snow in the upper reaches. Marty and I retreated to the cabin, where we kept a fire stoked and cooked soups right on the woodstove. When it was over, steelhead flooded into the river like convicts granted unexpected furlough, shooting upstream as far as they could go, chasing flies with hell-bent abandon and generally living it up before the chill of winter ordered them back into the confinement of deep, opaque pools. Vine maples and poison oak flared a bloody red, then went bare. Black-tailed bucks in the rut snorted and strutted like street toughs spoiling for a fight. But the true inheritors of the weather's thirst-slaking largesse, the real celebrants, were the mushrooms. Overnight they sprang from the sog as if on cue, a great fairy-tale crop of blooms in the dark woods, signaling the onset of the wet season.

After most of the season's chores had been seen to, I might have devoted every available moment to the river and its fish, snaking a steelhead fly through emerald pools. But the mushrooms came calling, and so I went on collecting missions closer to home. *Mushrooms Demystified*, the bible on the subject and a doorstop among field guides, accompanied me on these walks like a portly and garrulous uncle. Leafing through its hundreds of detailed pages, I lingered over the photographs of the author and his friends as much as those of the mushrooms themselves. They looked like Mendocino hippies who really did get back to the land and stayed there: goofy, earnest, with terrible haircuts and a lot of plaid, proudly holding up record-breaking morels. When not studying the pictures, I managed to learn a few of the basic families and genera and could reliably key out many of the often poetic-sounding species in our range: *Russula rosacea, Laccaria laccata, Ramaria rasilispora.*

Dozens of edible varieties fruited within walking distance of the cabin. Loose colonies of golden chanterelles (*Cantharellus formosus*) popped up in unlikely places, sometimes right under our noses: in moss behind the barn, beneath the twisted, flaking branches of manzanita along the driveway, in a dense stand of second-growth Douglas fir behind the cabin. We picked them regularly, starting out with small brown paper bags and graduating to cardboard produce boxes. White chanterelles (*Cantharellus subalbidus*)—larger, meatier, earthier—remained more of a mystery. They were harder to find and often required excavation. The best hunting ground was beneath the duff along the roadside and in a partially shaded spot among Pacific madrones and black oaks near the woodshed, where they hid under a thick mat of leaves. We went back to them repeatedly, like a squirrel checking on its nut caches.

Up the road the delicate black trumpet (*Craterellus cornucopioides*) lay concealed in tight clusters among moss and twigs. This relative of the chanterelle, also called horn-of-plenty or little black petunia, was hard to see, even in the open. More often than not it looked like a small hole in the ground. Sautéed lightly in butter, it tasted like fall.

Nearby, in well-drained washes of clay shaded by pine and fir, we found king boletes, those large, dome-headed mushrooms with spongy undersides so prized by Europeans. *Porcini*, the Italians call them: little pigs. To the Germans they are *steinpilz* and to the French, *ceps*. The scientific name, *Boletus edulis*, says it all:

superior edible mushroom. For hundreds of years, people from
Italy and Eastern Europe have taken to the woods in search of this
aromatic delicacy, eating it raw or cooked, and drying it to concentrate the earthy flavors for use in soups, stews, and sauces.

The king bolete's domain was an old overgrown skid road
near the irrigation pond, a place that never saw the sun. We
looked for it in its infancy, while it was still a dauphin and pushing its royal cap through the earth, before the parasitic flies could
get to it and lay their eggs. A worm-free bolete was cause for
celebration. We sliced them up and dried them on screens placed
beneath the wood-burning stove.

Always one to vaunt Martha's Polish-Italian blood, I took a
special liking to the boletes. It was comfort-food season, and I
felt it was my duty to make the cabin as comfortable as possible
with warm fires and the aromas of hearty meals. Marty had been
ill lately and slept much of the day on the couch. I stoked the fire
and made creamy mushroom pastas for her. Before long the rains
would turn to snow and the pass would close for the season. We
would need to make up our minds soon about whether to over-
winter in the cabin.

For me it was a simple choice. I was not ready to return to
the city. These months of caretaking the cabin had been perhaps
the happiest time of my life. I was spending nearly every waking
hour outdoors—chopping wood, clearing brush, maintaining
the road, working in the garden, fishing, hiking, and generally
soaking up every last ounce of the wilderness. According to our
agreement with the owners, we were obligated to stay on only
through October, but the idea of spending the winter in a place
apart, sequestered by the elements, appealed to me. And the
mushrooms, I was told, would fruit all winter long.

Mushrooms inspire varied and sometimes intense reactions
around the world. Neither plant nor animal, they inhabit a
kingdom that is otherworldly to most. Anglo-Saxons especially
view them with distrust. The woods are dark and deep in these

206 FAT OF THE LAND

cultures; it's no surprise that the English word toadstool, with its unpalatable overtones, is a common synonym for mushroom. In contrast, Mediterranean and Eastern European peoples have enjoyed a long, affectionate relationship with fungi. This was my model, and I decided that Martha's heritage granted me rights by association. I envisioned the warmth and camaraderie of the mushroom hunt: woven baskets overflowing with plump caps and stems; the scent of rich sauces wafting out of the kitchen; a sense of communion around the table that only dirty hands and foraged food can bring.

There was just one hitch: pick the wrong mushroom and you could die. If there is a single hard rule to observe, one golden and overarching dogma, it is this: never eat a mushroom you can't identify with certitude. And a corollary: it's more important to recognize the poisonous species than the edible ones. The vast majority of mushrooms are edible—if mostly bland, bitter, or otherwise unappetizing—but a select few are deadly, and these are the ones you should be able to recognize without a doubt if you plan to pick in the wild.

Amanita phalloides is a beautiful mushroom to behold. The cap, or pileus, is up to six inches in diameter, with a metallic green sheen that is striking when the mushroom is fresh. No skinny supermodel, it has a stem that is white and Rubenesque, giving this elegant mushroom a classic and proportional air, with a suggestion that it might just dance off into the duff. For all these reasons, it is a tempting siren of the forest floor. According to those who have eaten it—and lived to tell—it is also quite tasty.

Commonly known as the death cap, *A. phalloides* is responsible for more fatalities than any other species. It is thought that the death cap hitched a ride to North America from its native Europe, possibly hiding out among introduced nut trees or even seedlings that sowed the first cork plantations in California wine country, before spreading up and down the West Coast. Most poisonings in the United States are the result of a tragic case of mistaken identity: Southeast Asian immigrants sometimes deliberately pick and consume the death cap, believing it to be a mushroom found in their native land, the similar-looking paddy-straw mushroom (*Volvariella volvacea*). Over the years there have been many such poisonings. In 1988, a Korean-born woman living in Oregon served stir-fried *Amanita phalloides* to five dinner guests. Of the five, four required liver transplants. Those diners were lucky. Nearly every year someone in North America is delivered a fatal blow.

The death cap is a member of the most infamous of mushroom genera, *Amanita*. The destroying angel is another deadly *Amanita* with a catchy name. Because of its coloring—usually a ghostly white—it is less frequently mistaken for edible varieties, although in 2006 seven members of a Hmong community in Minnesota's Twin Cities were victimized by the destroying angel, including a ten-year-old girl who died. Many other species within the *Amanita* genus, several of which were common in our midst, are hallucinogenic and highly poisonous.

The toxins in these mushrooms are known as amatoxins, and they account for more than 90 percent of all mushroom-related fatalities. Amatoxins are absorbed directly into the bloodstream immediately after ingestion. They cannot be cooked out, dried out, or diluted. Unlike many toxins, amatoxins are not expelled through the urine; they continue to be recycled into the bloodstream. While some mildly poisonous mushrooms will give you gastric grief soon after ingestion, the amatoxins in truly deadly mushrooms usually don't make themselves known for six to twelve hours. After the initial latent period, symptoms can range from fierce abdominal pains and vomiting to diarrhea and severe weakness. This phase, which may last two to three days, is followed by an apparent recovery, during which the overt symptoms diminish. It is at this point, however, that the poison is working over the liver and kidneys. More than one patient has been released from the hospital seemingly on the mend, only to die a few days later. The final symptoms are jaundice, hypo-glycemia, hepatic coma, organ failure, and death. Patients lucky enough to recover without an organ transplant often require a month of hospital care and lifelong medication.

Nothing focuses the mind like an activity that might kill you. As the days got shorter and darker and wetter, and the steelhead fishing began to wane, I found myself spending more time stooped over in dank patches of woods, absorbed in a fungal classroom. At night I studied my day's catch so there would be no mistake. I brought home sacks of mushrooms and arranged them before me on newspapers spread across the kitchen table, *Mushrooms Demystified* at my side, sheets of white and black blotter and water glasses ready in case I needed a spore print. In the drama of the ID session, poisonous species became just as precious to me as edible ones. I studied and memorized them all.

In early October we had a tremendous fruiting of *Leccinum*, a type of bolete named for the diagnostic scabrous tufts on the stem. *Leccinum manzanitae* filled the pinewoods, and we took the best specimens to dry for wild mushroom risottos. In the mixed forest below the pond a fallen oak tree was host to the prized oyster mushroom, *Pleurotus ostreatus*, which we breaded and fried in butter as an appetizer.

Though we didn't find any of the deadliest specimens such as the death cap or the destroying angel, several poisonous *Amanitas* were common on the property, including *Amanita muscaria*, that archetypal toadstool resplendent in red with warty white polka dots across its cap, the mushroom so often depicted in the company of merry, red-hatted gnomes. Used for centuries by Native Americans in vision-questing rituals, *Amanita muscaria* is known to be unpredictable and dangerous but usually not fatal. Certain ethnobotanists believe that the nifty little Christian sideshow known as Santa Claus is plausibly descended from its use in the hallucinogenic rites of Siberian tradesmen. These nomadic peoples of the Far North, with their herds of reindeer, were known to have a taste for the psychoactive mushroom. Their reindeer had a yen for it too. Get it? Jolly man decked out in red and white. Flying reindeer. Ho ho ho. Some have even suggested that Jesus was part of a mushroom cult.

You don't have to believe that Christianity was kick-started by the first hippies to see the centrality of magic mushrooms to ritual behavior. Psychoactive plants and fungi have been used through the ages in tribal ceremonies to induce trancelike states, visions, and altered perception. The motive is clear: tap into a higher consciousness. Native Americans and other indigenous peoples around the world have known this for centuries. In the 1960s, the counterculture got a hold of psychoactive mushrooms and touted their ability to "open the doors of perception" and alter consciousness. Ingesting the magic mushroom was seen almost as a moral choice by its adherents, a way to steal a glimpse of true human potential and throw off the shackles of mindless conformity. These days, magic mushrooms are mostly used as a party stimulant.

Besides being Santa's favorite recreational drug, *Amanita muscaria* was the mind-altering mushroom preferred by Lewis Carroll, and science has since proven that the active ingredient, muscimol, is indeed responsible for inducing states of macropsia and micropsia—conditions in which objects appear to shrink or grow, as Alice experiences in Wonderland. But *A. muscaria*— also known as the "fly agaric" because it was used in ancient times to ward off insect pests—packs other toxins as well and is unpredictable.

Most modern vision questers have instead turned to a group of mushrooms known as psilocybes. While not deadly poisonous, the toxins in these potent little jobbers are sufficient to cause severe disorientation, loss of muscle coordination, and anxiety. They can also work on the body's neural chemistry to alter processes of the mind and enhance various modes of perception.

In her memoir of mushroom hunting, *Celebrating the Wild Mushroom*, Sara Ann Friedman traces the American public's introduction to psychoactive mushrooms to a 1957 *Life* magazine article by Gordon Wasserman, "In Search of the Magic

Mushroom," in which the author journeys to the Oaxacan highlands to find and experiment with psilocybes. "Partly because of Wasson," she writes, "and partly because of the growing use of LSD in the 1960s and the popularity of Carlos Castaneda, thousands of young people trooped off to Mexico searching for blue mushrooms in green pastures." For more recent generations, such pilgrimages have been obviated by the rise in domestic cultivation as well as the discovery that several species of psilocybin mushroom exist right in here in the U.S. of A., especially in the Northwest and Gulf Coast regions.

During my sophomore year in college in rural Vermont, a few of us decided to spend a day out in cow country hunting psychedelic mushrooms. It was mud season, that seemingly infinite shoulder time between winter and spring when the snow has mostly melted but the grass is definitely not green and not lustrous and not inviting to students who want nothing more than to get nearly naked and lie around on the quad with members of the opposite sex. No, this was a time of boots and sucking sounds coming from the earth. But we could feel a novel warmth of sun on our faces as we trudged to class through the puddles and mud pies. Bold crocuses tested the air. Tradition held that it would soon be time to gulp down a few dried caps and stems of the psilocybin mushroom and go wander, giggling, the remote corners of the greening campus—out past the graveyard to the amphitheater, perhaps, or beyond, to the lake and cliffs—with dilated pupils discreetly hidden behind shades.

Legend had it that the mushrooms in question commonly grew out of cow patties. We were looking for a type of psilocybe—something brownish and nondescript, as I recall, with maybe a little purple fringe or necklace. We traipsed about in some farmer's field, and sure enough, we found a lot of mushrooms, some of which even managed an ever so slight resemblance to our guidebook photos. These we stuck in gunnysacks and brought back to the dorm for drying. Somewhere along the line, though, someone—or all of us—lost the nerve, or started to question his ID skills, or simply forgot. The mushrooms moldered in a plastic bag at the bottom of a backpack, eventually dissolving into a soupy mess. Well, we all agreed days later, wiping our hands of the affair, so much for *that* experiment. The reality of wild mushrooms intervened in the end, and we defaulted to the common sense—or, at least, critical judgment—that a couple years of college had sort of given us.

In the third week of October, a fruiting of *Amanita* filled the woods. Clumps of it emerged all over the property—in the middle of the road, along the trails, right next to the cabin—and some were quite large. Like others in its genus, it grew out of a fleshy white, egglike case called a volva. The cap was bright orange, with a white skullcap on top, giving it the look of a yolk spilling from a cracked egg in its early stages of growth. It was a classic *Amanita*, no doubt about it, but it resembled several different species in our guidebook. We let it go at that. Many mushrooms went unidentified, lying limp on newspapers spread across the table, big question marks scrawled in laundry pen next to their rapidly decomposing bodies. Each night, when my eyes grew weary in the faint halo of propane light, I tossed the day's work off the deck for the deer browsing below.

   In any event, I was more focused now on finding edible species. Bradley, the owner of the cabin, was visiting in a few days, and he was bringing his mother to celebrate her ninety-second birthday. I promised that we would have a feast ready for them. Our downstream neighbors, Matt and Kate, were coming too. Though they lived only ten miles southwest of us as the crow flies, the drive would take them nearly two hours on rough logging roads. We jumped to prepare for the party. During a lull in the weather, I hiked down to the river and caught a seven-pound steelhead. The next day I headed upriver to the bend, where a few hatchery half-pounders fell for a Red Ant pattern in the fast water above the turn, the largest a bit over fifteen inches. A great blue heron watched me from its usual perch on a rock in the middle of the river, floating skyward once in alarm—or envy—as I played the first fish to shore. It settled back down with outstretched wings like a tented section of newspaper that has come to rest after a gust of wind. Hunched over, with its long beak held straight out, it eyeballed me from across the rapids as I gutted the three fish. The setting sun turned the river a dazzling orange, and even in death my young steelhead evinced a rosy hue. I left the offal on the rocks for the bird and made my way back to the trail.

Our patches continued to produce, too. A quarter mile up the driveway, at the head of a sharp curve just before the irrigation pond, an overgrown skid road disappeared into a thicket of tan oaks and manzanita. You walked down this path with your forearm out in front of you, fending off the branches in your face. At the end, several hundred yards away, was a landing—dark with fir saplings—where, more than thirty years ago, the cut timber had been stacked before being skidded back out to the road. Maybe all those trees piled up in one place had rubbed off their goodness on the land; the site was now carpeted golden yellow with the biggest, brightest chanterelles we had ever seen. Hundreds of them, most larger than a fist, twinkled like golden Christmas lights in the gloom. We set to them with abandon, filling our wine boxes with this extraordinary harvest. How had they grown to such proportion, we wondered. Was it too thick and brushy for the deer to bother? Did the bears conceivably not smell the earthy fecundity of a chanterelle garden?

The questions lingered in the moist air like a vapor. We switched on our headlamps and picked into the night in preparation for the meal, passing by the young and the old so the garden would thrive for another season, laughing and tripping over one another as we bent to the task of picking the freshest specimens, marveling at our magnificent gold strike.

It was raining again when our neighbors arrived. All smiles despite the downpour, Matt and Kate trooped in with cardboard boxes overflowing with some of the biggest mushrooms I had ever seen—the orange-capped *Amanitas* so ubiquitous on the property. Margery was right behind them, scooting along at a clip that could only be called rapid for a woman in her tenth decade, with her son Bradley on her heels. Margery had her own smaller flat of mushrooms. Flushed, with stained hands and knees and rain runneling off their hoods, the foursome had met on the road on the far side of the pass and driven in together. Halfway down the driveway they were compelled to pull over. "We hit the jackpot," Margery declared. Matt was already at work by the kitchen sink, trimming his mushrooms and paring away bits of dirt and pine needles. Little droplets of rain clung to his beard.

"What do you plan to do with all those?" I wanted to know.

Margery chortled, as if it wasn't obvious. "Eat them, I should think." She called it the biggest fruiting of *Amanita calyptrata* she had ever seen, and for a ninety-two-year-old card-carrying member of the Oregon Mycological Society, that was saying a lot. She had logged several decades' worth of fall mushroom seasons in the Rogue country, and she knew what she was talking about.

"What kind of mushroom did you say that was?"

"Don't look at me," Bradley said. "You all are the experts."

"Well, there is some dispute over the Latin name," Margery went on. "The mycologists haven't made up their minds. In any event, they're delicious." Matt explained that these were an edible kind of *Amanita*—a local delicacy, in fact—that was found in company with Pacific madrone. I said I didn't know there was such a thing as an edible *Amanita*.

"Quite to the contrary," replied Margery in her precise way. "Some of the choicest varieties are of the *Amanitae*. You simply need to be scrupulous and exercise care with your identification. The French will even eat *Amanita muscaria*, provided it's boiled and peeled."

"You're positive about these?"

"Of course."

The rain notwithstanding, our guests were all sunny as could be. Full buckets of wild mushrooms could have that effect. But the sight of those bright orange caps with white skullcaps being prepped for dinner left me uneasy. No one had more to lose than Martha. Recently all those fall days spent recuperating from a mystery illness on the couch had finally been explained with the help of a cheap pharmacy purchase and a follow-up doctor's appointment. As the blue end of the stick said—and the doctor confirmed—she was three months pregnant. We would not be spending the winter in the cabin. At any time, a cold wind might blow down from Alaska and crash into a moist front coming in off the Pacific—dumping snow at the higher elevations and closing the pass. The only way out was fifteen miles of trail and then a lucky ride from a remote trailhead. In some big snow years the pass didn't reopen until May. We were looking at a due date in late March or early April, give or take a few weeks.

Margery beckoned us over, a tattered first edition of *Mushrooms Demystified* on her lap and a few specimens limp on the table, one of them still encased in the white volval sac that is characteristic of the genus. She started to read aloud, then paused and turned one round in her hand. The cap was definitely orange and covered with a white patch that resembled a yarmulke. Margery raised her finger. "And here's an important point: *'margin usually clearly striate.'*" She showed us the fine striations that marked the outer edge of the cap.

"Usually?"

"They're not birds, dear." She cut one of our specimens lengthwise down the middle and passed a slice of stem around. Its hollow center and jelly filling were diagnostic. "I, for one, am looking forward to a delicious *Amanita* sauté."

Marty started to read. "Here's what it says about edibility: *'Too many people eat and enjoy the typical form for me not to recommend it. However, be absolutely sure of your identification.'*" She stopped reading without looking up.

"Don't take my word for it," said Margery. "You have to decide for yourself."

Italians call this mushroom *coccoli*, or "pampered baby."
In the Old World it's considered a delicacy, whether eaten raw
(sliced thin and drizzled with lemon and olive oil) or sautéed
with diced shallots and cooked in tomato sauce. Bradley held
up the specimen that Martha had been studying. "Your relatives
would know," he said to her, trying to lighten the mood.

Our downstream neighbors prepared the mushroom and kale
sauté while I got the barbecue going. Like us, Matt and Kate were
also in the process of packing up to drive out in advance of the
first winter snows. Since March they had been stationed at the
Rogue River Ranch near Marial, working for the Bureau of Land
Management to maintain the property and greet the many boaters who floated the Rogue's Wild and Scenic section and stopped
off to see the ranch's historical artifacts. The Billings family
had homesteaded the ranch, and the original house was now a
museum. It had been built in the colonial style, was painted a
spiffy red, and displayed many original hand-hewn tools and
other facets of pioneer life. Matt and Kate worked as the museum
docents. They were also charged with keeping a very large garden on the property to show off the river valley's fertile soils. To
the kale, which came from their garden, they added the chopped
mushrooms and plenty of garlic and soy sauce. My steelhead fillets were marinating in a light Asian sauce, awaiting the grill; the
half-pounders would be pan-fried whole with butter and herbs.
    Though it would be foolish to think our interlude off the
grid approached anything like that faced by the first home-
steaders—we had propane, after all, to fuel a refrigerator, stove,
and lanterns—the food was not appreciably different from that
of a hundred years earlier. Kippered steelhead and chunks of
cold-smoked chinook from a thirty-pound hen I had caught in
July made the rounds. Bradley passed crackers dolloped with a
homemade caviar of chinook roe from a fish he had taken on the
Salmon River near Tillamook. "My mother caught two that same
day," he said loudly so Margery could hear. "A ninety-one-year-

old woman hauling in a twenty-pound salmon. Imagine that!"

"You gaffed it alongside the boat and tailed it for me," she corrected. Bradley grinned.

"What? Am I not supposed to lend a hand to my own mother?"

The cocktail hour went on for a while, with Bradley mixing up his famous boat drinks, using handfuls of fresh mint and a lot of gin. Raucous cowboy music played in the background. More drinks appeared. The gathering was loose and boisterous. Marty and I hurried in and out of the kitchen, checking on the food. The dinner table was just large enough to seat us all, with an ornate kerosene lamp as its centerpiece. I brought the fish out on a platter. Marty presented a large bowl of garden-fresh tomato-zucchini stew, along with a dish of wild rice and another wooden bowl of salad picked moments earlier by flashlight. The kale-mushroom concoction came out last, and everyone dug in.

As the dinner progressed, with one local delicacy after another circling the table, each course complemented by an arsenal of home brews, wines, and spirits, I started to get that peculiar sense of nervous energy and pent-up anxiety that is prelude to a mushroom trip. It was a feeling I recognized right away. Outside, the rain washed over the canyon in a light drizzle and the sky was black. Inside, the kerosene lamp cast an eerie glow that lit up our faces and reached into the corners of the cabin with thin fingers of light. Shadows of gesticulating hands and arms played on the ceiling beams. For a moment I thought I was seeing the energy of objects as they moved through the air, like the tail of a comet. We called these tracers in college. I decided to not say anything. Everyone was laughing and telling stories—no need to make them suddenly paranoid. I braced myself for what I was sure would be a long and potentially off-kilter night. Just wait, I said to myself, they'll feel the *Amanitas* in a minute.

Something about the light in the rafters, the way it played off the beams and exposed patterns in the wood grain, reminded me of an early experience with psychoactive mushrooms. It had been an uneventful Saturday night in the dorm. Someone produced a baggie with several dried, innocuous-looking caps and stems. We forced them down with peanut butter and beer to mask the musty taste, and then waited. Nothing happened. It was snowing outside. Tom Bailey, a clean-cut boy from Nashville with small black eyes and perfect black hair—a devotee of the Velvet Underground and Goo Goo Clusters, which he had mailed to him from Tennessee—started talking about his summer job as a tour guide at the Grand Ole Opry. At some point in the story he was standing on a table and delivering his spiel from memory. We laughed without restraint, rolling in the aisles of the South's most famous concert hall. The room inhaled and exhaled. "I think it's working," someone was whispering. Snow pelted the tall plate-glass windows and caught the nimbus of candlelight inside, the barrier between inside and outside melting away as gusts whirled around the streetlamps like a mad swarm of insects and lights and shadows faced off in the rafters. Musical notes floated down from dorm rooms above like softly landing flakes of snow. Tom Bailey's deep southern voice rose in a crescendo. "And now, ladies and gentlemen, the lovely Dolly Parton…"

"More 'shrooms?" Bradley asked me.

Waving him off, I wondered how far down the rabbit hole these *Amanitas* would take us. I steeled myself. And then, just like that, the nervous energy dissipated. I gathered my wits and enjoyed another glass of wine and offered a toast. Margery was in a jovial mood. She told stories of canyon life from the old days— about a kleptaholic crow named Sam, who pilfered fishing gear from anglers as they floated past Black Bar; about the time Doc was summoned to perform emergency surgery on a Brit who had stuck himself in the eye with a double hook, how he practiced all night on an apple before successfully removing the two hooks, barbs and all; about the mail carrier Hathaway Jones, the one with the harelip who, in his sibilant voice, told tall tales about world-record melons and pole-vaulting bears.

The momentary tremors in the firmament had passed, and

there was no explaining it. The mushrooms, for their part, tasted delicious, almost like fried seafood. As best as I could guess, my subconscious—or maybe even some little known property of the mushrooms themselves, perhaps of all mushrooms—had summoned a minor flashback from days gone by. I looked at Martha. Her face was round and fair, her cheeks red in the warmth of camaraderie and lamplight, and I detected just the slightest bit of pudge in her midsection. *Coccoli.* She laughed boisterously at some joke that went over my head and then caught my gaze. "A-ma-ni-ta," she whispered slowly, letting the syllables take on their own weight.

CREAMY CHANTERELLE PASTA

It would be irresponsible of me to offer anything in the way of an Amanita recipe, but rest assured that this creamy chanterelle pasta is a frequent request of my dinner guests. You can use store-bought cremini mushrooms, but this dish is far superior with fresh chanterelles, which offer a fruity counterpoint to the bacon, and it's nearly as good with chanterelles that have been previously sautéed and frozen, so you can eat it in the depths of a cold, dark winter, when the chanterelles in the northern latitudes have long since returned to the earth. Green peas add a dash of color.

4 tablespoons (½ stick) butter
4 slices (¼ pound) thick, quality bacon,
    diced (or the equivalent of pancetta)
1–2 shallots, finely chopped
1 pound shaped pasta (I prefer bow ties)
1 pound fresh chanterelles (or the equivalent frozen)
Salt and freshly ground black pepper to taste
1 pint heavy cream (or less)
4 ounces garden peas, fresh or frozen
½ cup grated Parmesan, with more for the table

Preheat oven to 250 degrees. In a large skillet, heat 2 tablespoons of the butter over medium heat and add the diced bacon. Do not drain fat. As bacon begins to crisp, add shallots and cook until tender, a few minutes. Meanwhile, bring a pot of water to a boil and add pasta. Add chanterelles to skillet and cook several minutes, stirring occasionally, until they have released their water. Season with salt and pepper. In a large glass or ceramic mixing bowl, add remaining 2 tablespoons of butter and half the cream. Place mixing bowl in warm oven. Slowly add remaining cream to skillet and simmer, continuing to stir occasionally while pasta cooks. When pasta is nearly done, add peas to chanterelle sauce. Remove pasta from heat, drain, and pour into warmed mixing bowl. Mix in sauce along with grated Parmesan and serve immediately. If you're worried about all that cream and butter, open an extra bottle of red wine. SERVES 4

ACKNOWLEDGMENTS

MANY TALENTED INDIVIDUALS contributed time and exper-
tise to this book, whether in the field, the kitchen, or the office.
I am grateful for the insight and steady hand of my editor Kate
Rogers, for Sherri Schultz's keen eye, Isolde Maher's lovely illustrations, Mayumi Thompson and Jane Jeszeck's collaborative
design work, Shanna Knowlton's enthusiasm, and my agent Peter
McGuigan's support and confidence. I would not have gotten
anywhere without good advice in the early stages: many thanks
to Steve Duda for all that red ink spilled during long sessions at
the Jolly Roger Tap Room; to Kitty Harmon for steering me in
the right direction when the time came; and to Debbie Reber for
helping me put my best foot forward. PEN Northwest, overseer
of the Margery Boyden Wilderness Writing Residency, has my
sincerest gratitude for providing me with both a truly unique
place to work and for introducing me to the Boyden brothers—
Bradley and Frank—who have taught me so much about the art
of living well in the bush.

    This book would not have been possible without the host of
good friends and relatives who willingly joined me for outdoor
adventures, at some risk to their own health and reputations,
or ate my food, some of it not ready for prime time. You know
who you are. To those who make appearances in these pages, I
cherish your skill and companionship: Joe Hoskins (aka Warpo);

Chris and Lori Cora; David Francis and Lesley Zavar. To the fearless test kitchen cooks, *salute*: Becky Selengut, April Pogue, Amy Pennington, Traca Savadogo, Naomi Bishop, Brett Tomky, Naomi Andrade Smith, Janna Wemmer. Also, I extend my deep appreciation to Jeremy Faber, professional forager, for generously sharing his knowledge and to Kristin Hyde, consultant with Good Food Strategies, who helped me better understand the politics of what we eat.

Finally, I'd like to acknowledge my parents, who provided me with more opportunity than I can enumerate here, and my wife Martha Silano. At our wedding, my friend Addy offered a toast in which he extolled Marty for rescuing me from a life of juvenilia and endless cans of Chef Boyardee. That was some time ago, and I like to think I've shown improvement. Throughout the writing of this book, Marty offered unceasing encouragement and close reading while enduring the particular privations of being married to an itinerant hunter-gatherer, and for all that, I am truly thankful.